Birds—With a Magic Brush

Contents

Birds—With a Magic Brush

Beautiful, exciting—best of all, easy even for the beginner—birds are the perfect subjects to paint! Bring the wonderful world of nature indoors and grace your home with the natural beauty of our feathered friends. Choose from the stately Canada Goose, the Mallard, your favorite songbirds—or even the majestic Bald Eagle. And while you paint, learn more about these special creatures who share our world.

The TV Series "BIRDS—WITH A MAGIC BRUSH" shows just how easily birds—beautiful ones!—can be painted. Anyone can learn Sherry Nelson's unique color placement methods. Try YOUR hand at painting magnificent, graceful birds—as realistic as those outside your window.

Never picked up a brush? Can't draw a straight line? Don't worry—the methods you will learn here will make birds appear like magic from your palette! Come on—join the folks who have learned to create realistic birds with brush and paint. Create a painting you can hang in your home and take pride in. Have YOU always wanted to paint? Sherry can make that dream come true!

Rick Truhn, Publisher
DECORATIVE ARTS DIGEST

Sherry was the feature artist in September 1986.

DECORATIVE ARTS DIGEST is a monthly magazine you will want to receive. Each month you will see the same high quality color reproduction and instructive articles that make BIRDS—WITH A MAGIC BRUSH such a great book. Sherry C. Nelson is a regular contributor with a monthly, informative column. Periodically DECORATIVE ARTS DIGEST presents a new painting done by Sherry especially for you.

Well-known artists from around the world create paintings that will help you enjoy painting. You will also enjoy meeting new artists and learning different art techniques and styles with each new issue of DAD.

Some of those attending the 1st Seminar Extravaganza in Orlando, Florida.

To keep informed of seminars, workshops, and special travel/vacation seminars with Sherry, subscribe today to DECORATIVE ARTS DIGEST. You will enjoy the variety of articles, in addition to looking at a beautiful magazine.

Write: Decorative Arts Digest
P.O. Box 13371A
Orlando, FL 32859 **or call 305-841-7466**

Let's Talk About Supplies

Twenty-two different oil colors were used to create the 13 paintings in this book. You do not have to acquire them all at once. I would suggest that you pick several of your favorite birds and purchase the colors needed for them to help ease your budget. The abbreviations shown are used throughout the text. Try to become familiar with them.

Certain colors may be found only in a particular brand. Your art supplier can help you find the colors you will need and make correct substitutions if necessary.

CYL—Cadmium Yellow Light
B—Ivory Black
W—Titanium White
BU—Burnt Umber
RU—Raw Umber
UB—Ultramarine Blue
M—Mauve
MB—Mars Brown

RS—Raw Sienna
YO—Yellow Ochre
WO—Winsor Orange
PG—Permanent Green
BR—Bright Red
BS—Burnt Sienna
CO—Cadmium Orange

VDB—Van Dyke Brown
CYM—Cadmium Yellow Medium
CRL—Cadmium Red Light
WG—Warm Gray
COxG—Chromium Oxide Green
ChD—Chrome Yellow Deep
CS—Cadmium Scarlet

You will also need the following sizes of **Red Sable** brushes:

#2 Bright, #4 Bright, #6 Bright, #8 Bright and a #1 Round brush that comes to a fine point. The "Brights" have a shorter bristle length than "flats" and are better for the fine lines and sharp edges we will be doing.

And remember, good quality brushes and paints are an investment and are essential. You cannot paint to the best of your ability with a brush that will not hold a good chisel edge—or with paint that does not have sufficient pigment to hold a true color. Pay for quality materials, take the best of care of them, and you will save much frustration and money in the long run.

Additional items you will need are the following:

- Disposable palette for oil paint
- Odorless turpentine or brush cleaner for cleaning brushes and for thinning paint.
- Graphite paper for transfering designs to painting surface
- Paper Towels

Jar acrylic paints, clear acrylic spray and cheesecloth for preparation of painting surfaces. See SIMPLE BACKGROUNDS, P. 6.

Color Placement Sheets

This wonderful invention will help you apply colors correctly where you want them and insure that your birds turn out beautifully. AND they will make painting SO easy for you!

PLACEMENT 1—Shows the areas to be basecoated and where space allows the colors to be used in basecoating those areas as well.

PLACEMENT 2—Shows areas of color, commonly known as shading, highlighting or feather detail. These colors are applied on top of the colors blocked in during the Placement 1 step.

Simple abbreviations are used on the placement sheets:

B/ or BASE/	means to "basecoat" or to fill in the area entirely with color indicated.
S/ or Sh/ or SHADE/	means to "shade" or *deepen the basecoat* with the color indicated.
HL/ or HIGHLIGHT/	means to "highlight" or to *lighten the basecoat* with the color indicated.
xxx	X's indicate the location of highlights *on top of the basecoat.*
D/ or DARK/	means a dark mix used to partially basecoat an area as indicated.
L/ or LIGHT/	means a light mix used to partially basecoat an area as indicated.

Now let's look at some examples:

B/ RU	means to basecoat the area shown with Raw Umber.
S/ BU	means to deepen the basecoat where indicated, usually by a dotted line, with Burnt Umber.
HL/ CYL+W	means to lighten the basecoat where shown by xx's with a mixture of Cadmium Yellow Light and Titanium White.
B/ B	A trick? Not at all. Simply means basecoat with Ivory Black.

You might wish to review color abbreviations at this point . . . see listing of colors under LET'S TALK ABOUT SUPPLIES. And with the terminology behind us, let's take a look at . . .

Written Instructions

More detailed written instructions are included for each painting. They tie it all together, detailing the step-by-step methods you'll need to use as well as spelling out any colors not indicated on placement sheets because of space limitations. Refer to the written instructions often—not just to the color charts.

Color Photographs

Your guide to the finished product. But remember—in painting a lot of variation is desirable and natural. Neither your painting nor your handwriting will be exactly like mine! The birds we will paint vary in countless ways as well, with plumage differences from year to year as well as from summer to winter. Use the color plates as a guide but don't worry unduly about every last feather!

We at Cody Publications, Inc. have produced top-notch quality printing for many years and are proud of the excellent craftsmen we have working for us. Fortunately, they also are human. If they weren't, who could deal with them.

We also admit our mistakes when we make them and that's why we're alerting you that WE GOOFED on pages 5, 10 and 15.

This insert has those pages as they should have been printed. We apologize for the errors and sincerely hope they have not caused you any serious inconvenience.

Walt Willis
Cody Publications, Inc.

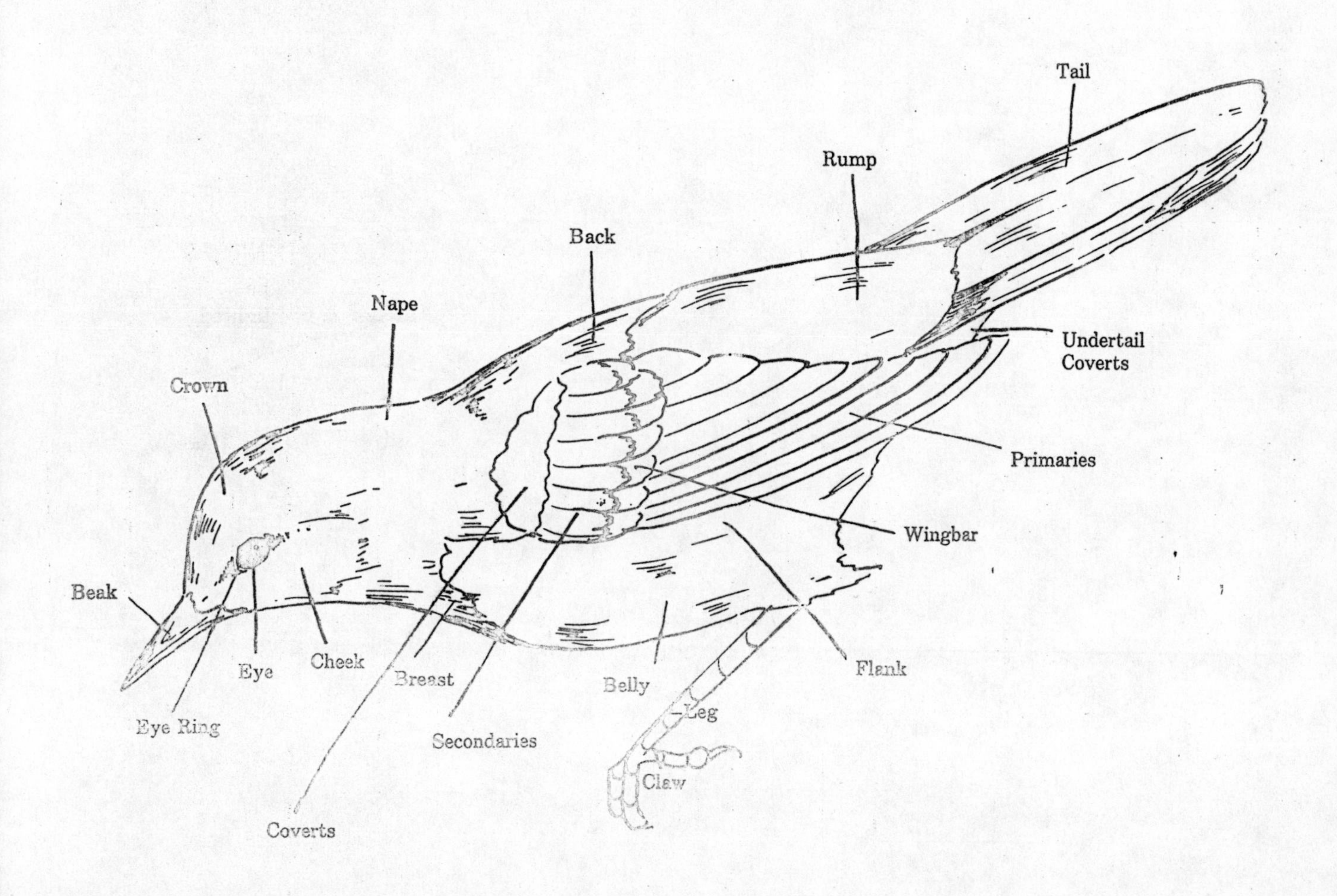

The Snow Bunting

What better setting for a Snow Bunting than a snowy branch on a gray winter day? Just looking at this little bird huddled against the snow makes me cold! I can almost feel the icy air and the wind-driven snow, can't you? In winter plumage, the Snow Bunting has rusty and browns to its feathers; by Spring this color has worn away, leaving the bird in its crisp black and white breeding garb! If you live in the Northern half of the country, you should be familiar with the "snow bird."

The background for the Bunting is an 8″ × 10″ masonite panel, painted with a soft gray. After a spray of matte acrylic, the out-of-focus look was created with splotches of WG, RU and W. Apply the colors, blending them into the background gray with cheesecloth and a light touch. Blend the darker colors first, then the W. When dry, respray and apply design with graphite paper.

Colors needed for this design: Raw Umber, Raw Sienna, Titanium White, Ivory Black and Chromium Oxide Green.

You will also need a #6 bright and a #1 round brush.

THE SNOW BUNTING

Wings: Base / RU. Streak in light feather lines with W.

Breast: Base / W. Shade with RU and RS where indicated. Highlight with W on liner brush for increased texture and interest, especially in areas of xx's.

Head: Base crown with RU, sparsely, as well as cheek line. Base remainder of area with W. Blend edges of RU into W carefully; do not overblend. Then with liner add texture, first with W, then with RU to deepen in front and behind eye.

Eye: Base / B. Highlight with point of round brush and a dot of W.

Beak: Base / RU. HL / W.

BRANCH

Apply RU in back and forth "skizzle" motion with chisel edge of brush. Then highlight with W. Rub colors into background just a little to soften. Allow background color to show through here and there for another value. Then add snow, rather thickly, with W along top edge of branch.

NEEDLES

Thin a mixture of COxG + a little B. Pull on needles with round brush. Start at branch and pull brush outward. If needles tend to be too fat, the mixture of paint is probably not thin enough. Then, with chisel edge of flat brush, add a little W between needles where snow is building up.

Finish up any last minute details, sign your name and then get ready to make "snow"! Thin a little W paint on the palette, touch the bristles of an old toothbrush in the mixture and spatter it onto the surface by pulling thumbnail across bristles—or flat blade of a palette knife. Careful! It is easy to get a blizzard when you only wanted a flurry . . . and try to keep most of the "snow" around the bird, not on it!

Pictured in color on page 17.

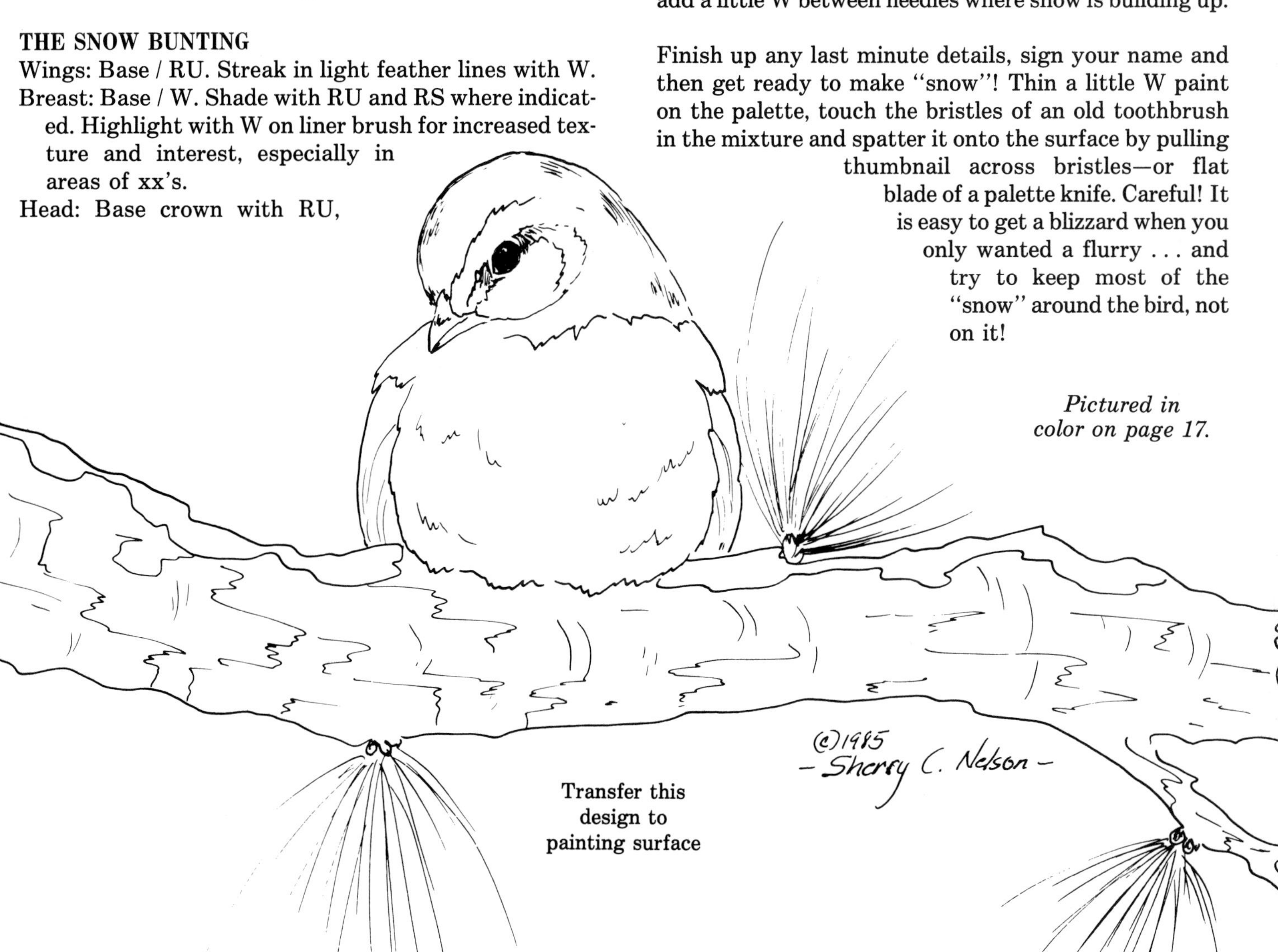

Transfer this design to painting surface

The Snow Bunting

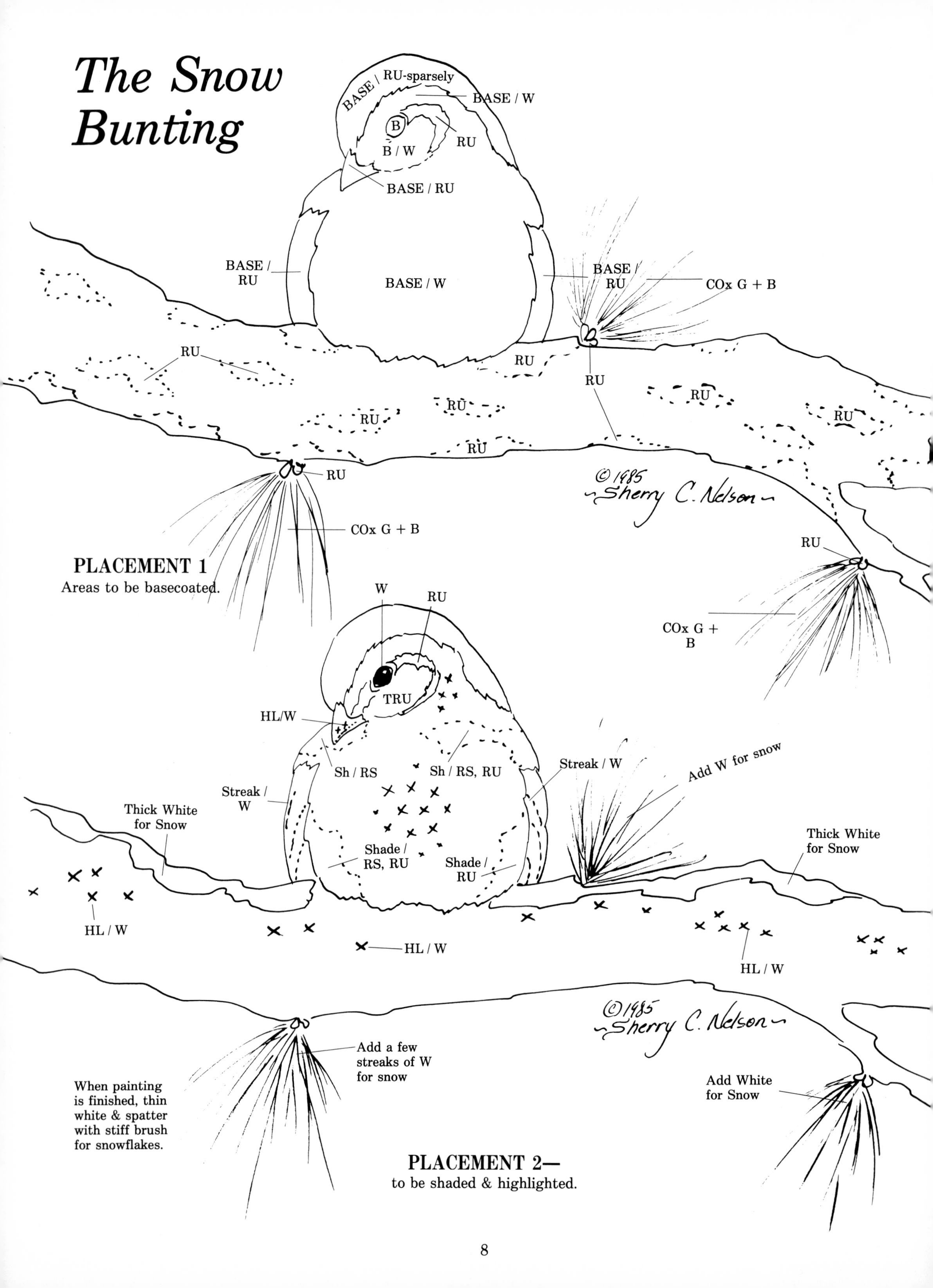

American Goldfinch

The Goldfinch is another popular bird at window-side feeders, lured in by offerings of their favorite food, the seed of the thistle. In fact, so well-known is this preference that in early American folk art the stylized representation of a small yellow bird was known as the "Distlefink" or "Thistlefinch." Small flocks of Goldfinches may be seen throughout the continent, searching out seeds of sunflowers, chicory, dandelions—and the ever-favorite thistle.

The 8″ × 10″ background panel for the Goldfinch painting is a piece of masonite painted with antique white acrylic and sprayed with matte finish acrylic spray. The accent splotching is done with Raw Umber oil paint to give the additional interest needed.

The colors needed for this design are the following: Mauve, Ivory Black, Titanium White, Cadmium Yellow Light, Chrome Yellow Deep, Raw Umber and Raw Sienna.
You will also need a #6 bright and a #1 round brush.

Pictured in color on page 18.

Transfer this design to painting surface.

THE GOLDFINCH

Tail and Wing feathers: Base/ B. As feather lines are covered with paint, etch lines into wet paint with handle of brush. Then using etched lines as a guide, add feather lines with W on chisel edge of brush. Blend W wingbar across upper portion of wing slightly upward into B paint.
Then set in W feather lines for that section.

Shoulder patch:
Base / CYL + W.

Belly and Rump: Base / W.

Breast, shoulder and cheek:
Base / ChD. Highlight where indicated with xx's with CYL + W, and then straight W.

Crown: Base / B. Highlight / W.

Beak: Base / RS. Shade / RU. Highlight / W.

Eye: Base / B. Highlight / W.

Leg: Base / RS. Shade RU. Highlight with W. Do detail segment lines with B.

THISTLE STEM AND BRACT

Base / CYL + B. Highlight / CYL + W.

THISTLE

Thin Mauve paint, then apply fine lines of blossom with round brush. If lines are too heavy, thin paint more and hold brush more upright. Highlight in central portion of blossom with thinned W, also applied with round brush.

American Goldfinch

We at Cody Publications, Inc. have produced top-notch quality printing for many years and are proud of the excellent craftsmen we have working for us. Fortunately, they also are human. If they weren't, who could deal with them.

We also admit our mistakes when we make them and that's why we're alerting you that WE GOOFED on pages 5, 10 and 15.

This insert has those pages as they should have been printed. We apologize for the errors and sincerely hope they have not caused you any serious inconvenience.

Walt Willis
Cody Publications, Inc.

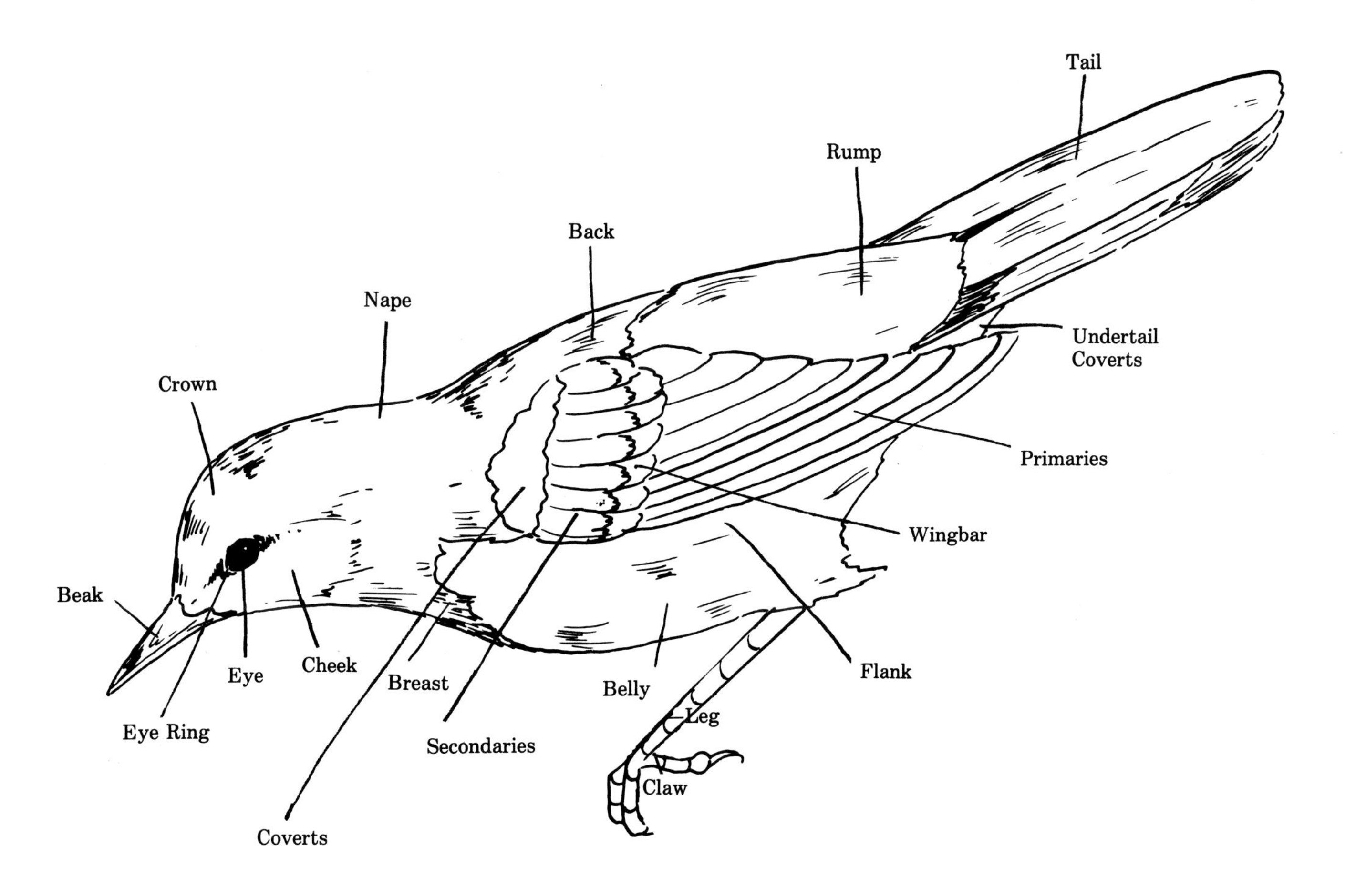

American Goldfinch

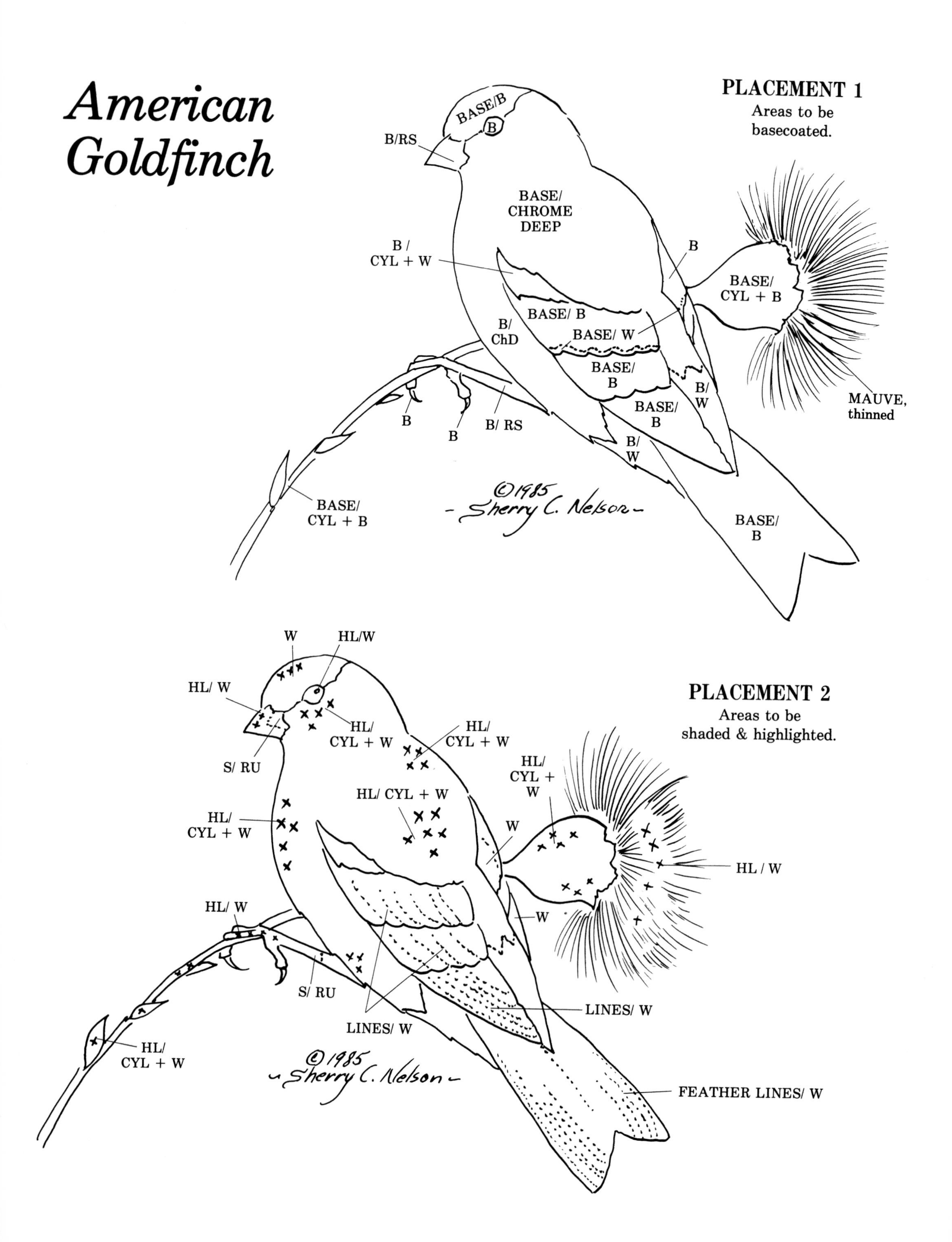

Black-capped Chickadee

Though a woodland bird, the wonderful little Chickadee is more often seen on the backyard feeders throughout the Northern United States. They are gentle, tame, and friendly, occasionally coming to feed from an outstretched hand. One of America's most popular birds, this jauntily-dressed acrobat has been chosen as the state bird of two states, Maine and Massachusetts. Even painting this special bird is enough to put you in high spirits and good humor!

The 9″ × 12″ masonite panel which forms the surface for the Chickadee painting is painted with soft gray acrylic paint and sprayed with matte finish acrylic spray. It is then accented with RU + COxG as well as W to give it depth and the unique out-of-focus look. The effect is that of a wintry sky—a perfect setting for the perky bird.

Colors used in this painting are the following: Warm Gray, Chromium Oxide Green, Ivory Black, Raw Umber and Titanium White. Brushes used are the #6 or #8 bright and the # round.

THE CHICKADEE

Tail: Base/ WG + RU. Mixture should be about 1-1 in proportion. Shade at top of tail area if needed with additional dark. Streak in feather lines with W.

Wings: Base/ WG + RU. Etch feather lines into wet paint with wooden handle of brush, then set them in with chisel edge of flat brush and W paint.

Shoulder: Base/ WG + RU + W. Highlight with W where indicated with xx's

Breast: Base according to placement sheet, dark half with WG + RU + W and the light area with W. Blend lightly where they meet to soften colors together. Highlight with additional W.

Transfer this design to painting surface.

Pictured in color on page 19.

Black-capped Chickadee

Cheek: Base/ W. Shade with RU + WG. Highlight with W.
Black Cap: Base/ B. Edge into white areas around it with corner of brush. Do not blend, just connect the colors.
Eye: Base/ B. Highlight/ W.
Beak: Base/ B + RU. Highlight where shown with W.
Leg: Base/ RU + WG. Highlight down shaft of leg with W. Add detail lines with B on round brush as shown on design.

BRANCH
Dark/ RU. Light/ W. Block in colors according to placement sheet. "Skizzle" colors together: use chisel edge of brush and slide with length of branch in short strokes, from light to dark to achieve a choppy, textured, bark-like blend.

NEEDLES
Thin B + COxG, apply needles with round brush. If needles are too fat, mixture needs to have additional turp added to make it a bit thinner. Then thin a little W and add a few white needles for interest.

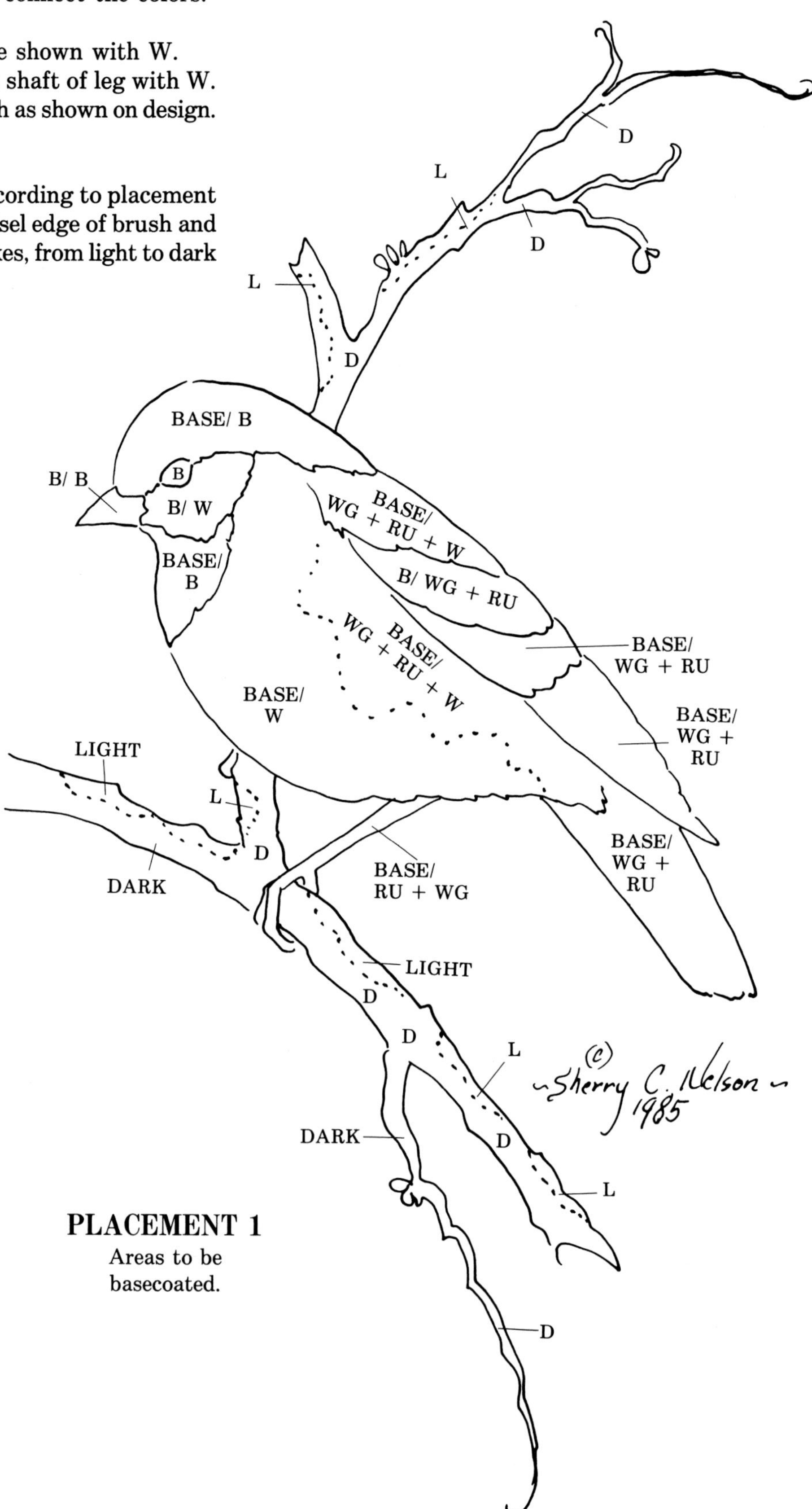

PLACEMENT 1
Areas to be basecoated.

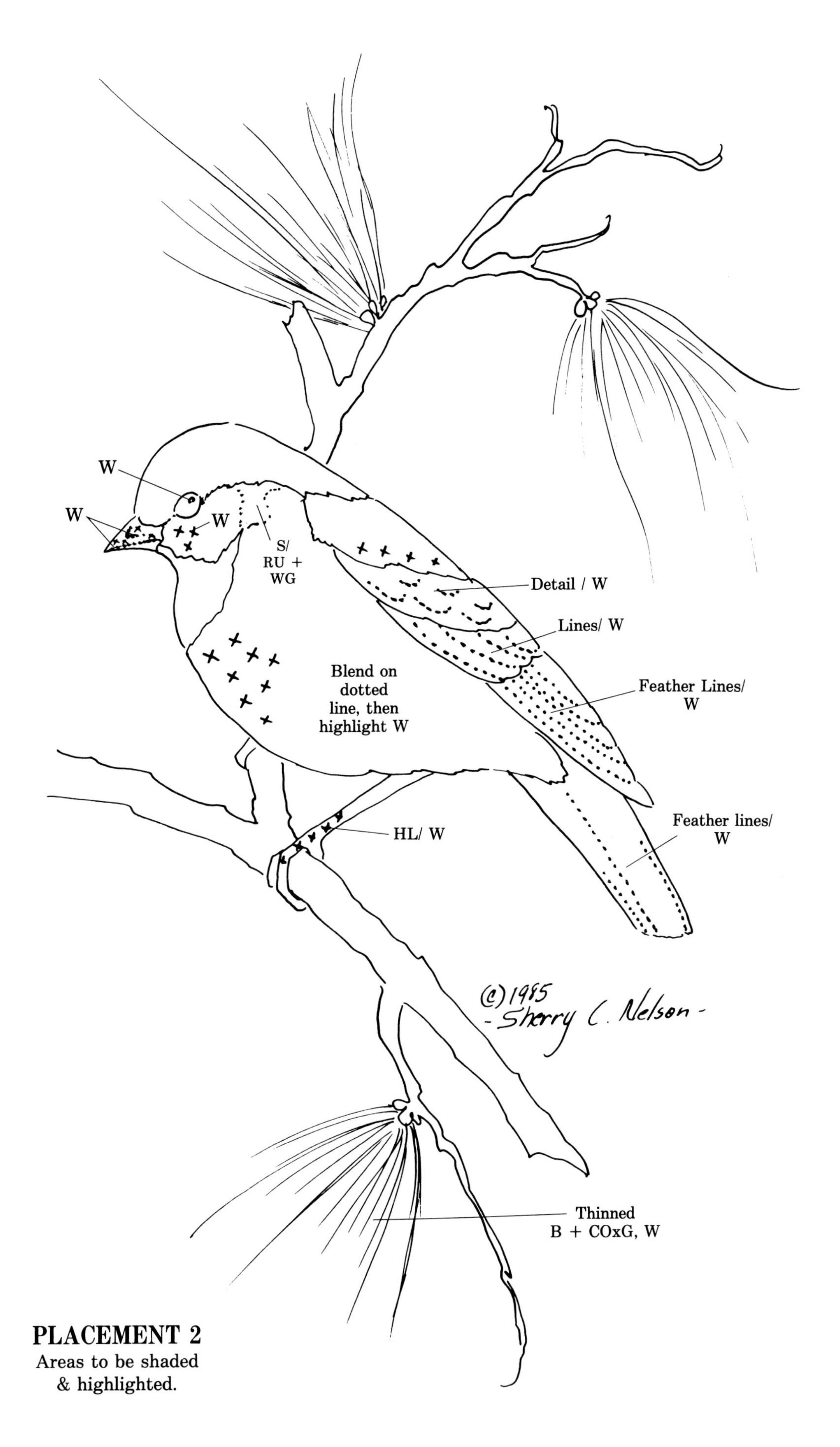

PLACEMENT 2
Areas to be shaded
& highlighted.

Northern Oriole

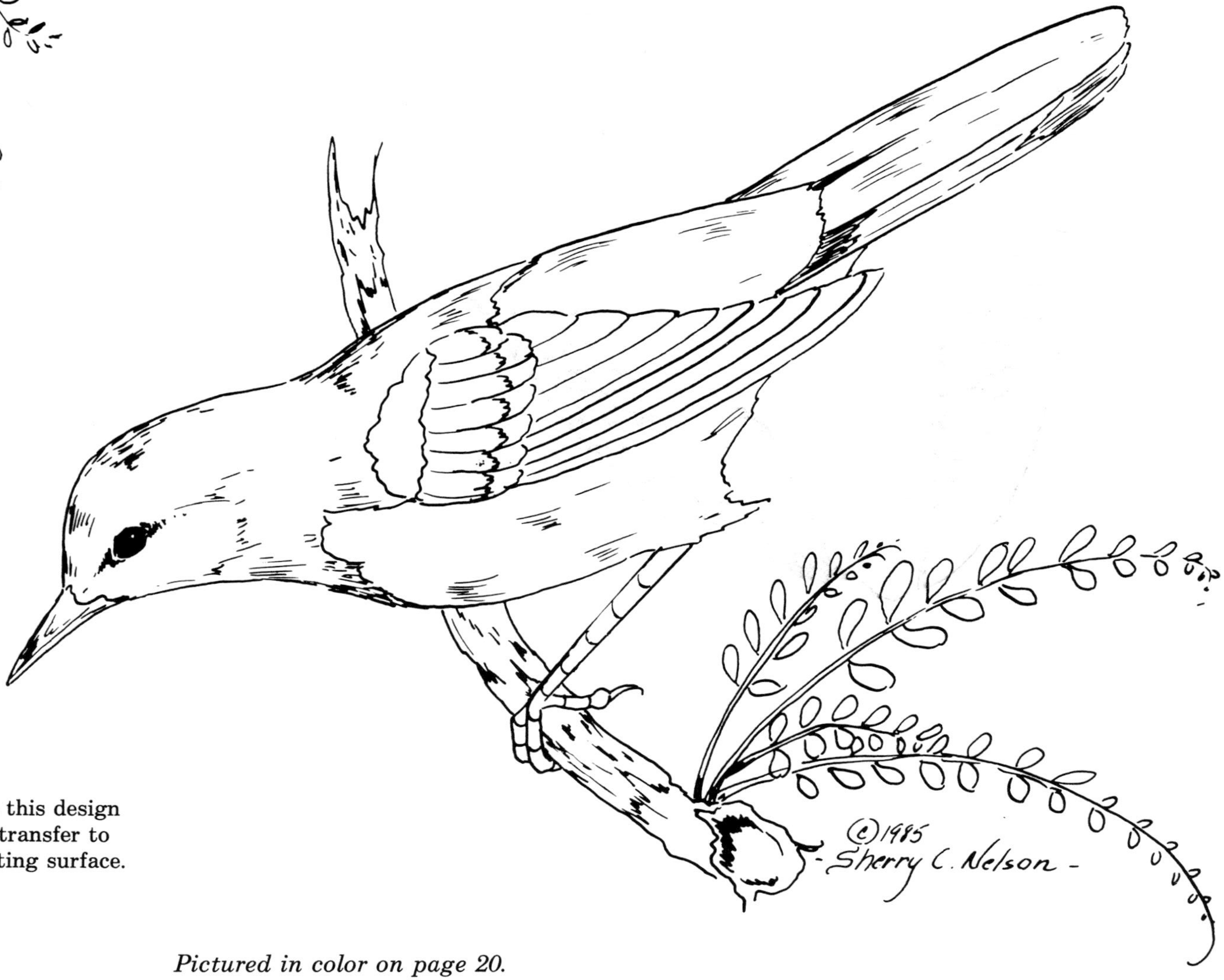

©1985
Sherry C. Nelson

Use this design
to transfer to
painting surface.

Pictured in color on page 20.

Northern Oriole

Known in the East as the Baltimore Oriole and in the West as the Bullock's, the two birds comprise a single species: the Northern Oriole. The ranges of the two subspecies overlap on the Great Plains, and one or the other may be found throughout the United States. The female Northern Oriole is one of the most skillful builders of any bird, constructing a complex hanging nest of plant fiber, strings, and grass. Attached to a slender branch, the swaying sack-like construction is truly an incredible creation. This painting depicts the flashy male, an enjoyable addition to your collection of favorite bird paintings.

The 9″ × 12″ masonite background is painted with antique white acrylic which has been sprayed with matte finish and antiqued with splotches of RU oil paint. With the brush, apply oil paint, unthinned, and rub and buff into background panel with cheesecloth. When dry, respray and apply design.

The colors used are the following: Raw Umber, Burnt Umber, Ivory Black, Titanium White, Cadmium Orange and Cadmium Yellow Light. Use the following brushes: #8 bright and #1 round.

THE ORIOLE

Tail: Base / B + BU in the dark areas and with CO in the orange areas. Add feather lines with W in the dark areas and with B in the orange areas.

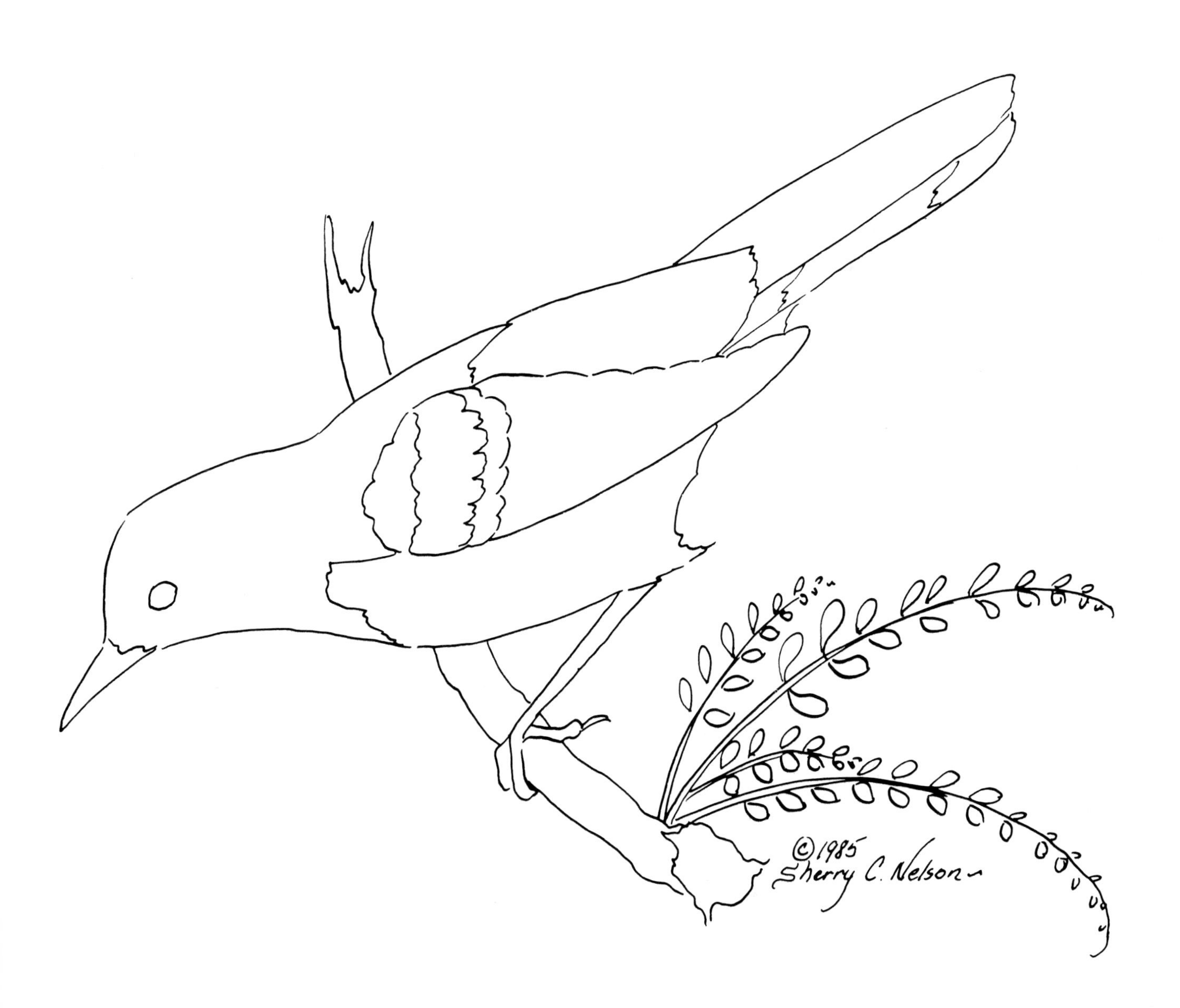

Northern Oriole

Primary wing feathers: Base / B + BU. Etch feather lines into wet paint with handle of brush, then paint in with W.

Wingbar: B / W.

Secondary feathers, above wingbar: Base / B + BU. Using chisel edge of brush, slightly blend the light band into the dark area. Then add feather lines with W.

Breast, Back and Shoulder: Base / CO. Shade where indicated with RU. HL / CYL + W in areas of xx's.

Head, neck: Base / B + BU. Highlight these dark areas with W, giving just a sheen of light color.

Eye: Base / B. Outline with a dark gray mix of B + W. Then highlight eye with W.

Beak: Dark / B + BU. Light / W. Blend just a little between color areas.

Leg: Base / B + RU. Shade / RU. Highlight / W. Overall look should be a pale gray. Then add claws and segment lines with pointed brush and B paint.

BRANCH:
Base with sparse RU. Highlight with a little W.

STEMS:
Base / B + CYL.

LEAVES:
Thin a mixture of CYL + B and make tiny strokes for leaves with tip of round brush. Increase pressure on brush for larger leaves and decrease it for the tiny ones.

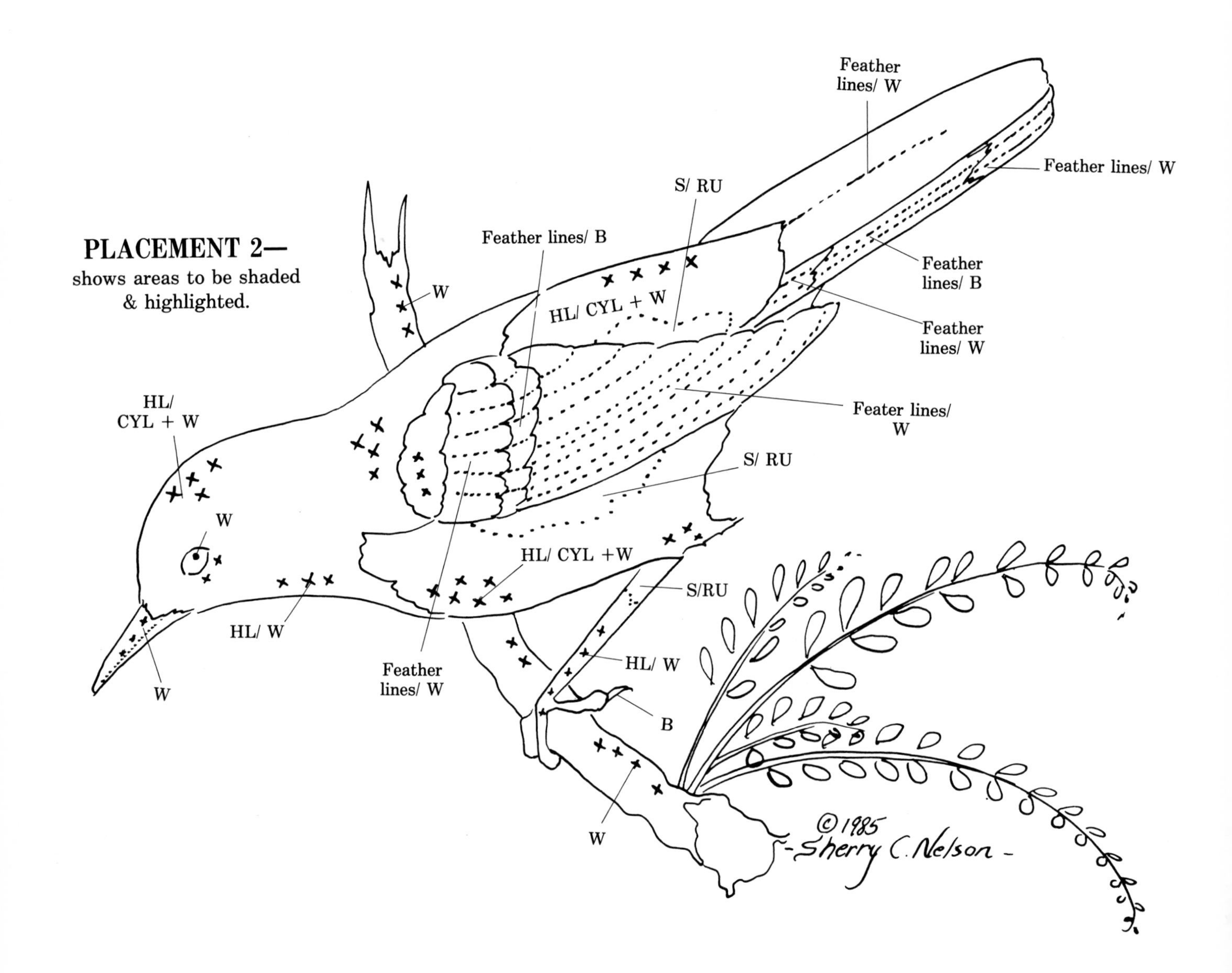

The Snow Bunting

Instructions begin on page 7.

American Goldfinch

Instructions begin on page 9.

Black-capped Chickadee

Instructions begin on page 11.

Sherry C. Nelson 1985

Northern Oriole

Instructions begin on page 14.

Red-headed Woodpecker

Instructions begin on page 33.

The Common Loon

Instructions begin on page 36.

Sherry C. Nelson 1985

Eastern Bluebird

Instructions begin on page 40.

Taping of TV Series

The Mallard

Instructions begin on page 43.

American Robin

Instructions begin on page 46.

The Northern Cardinal

Instructions begin on page 49.

The Canada Goose

Instructions begin on page 52.

Ring-billed Gull

Instructions begin on page 58.

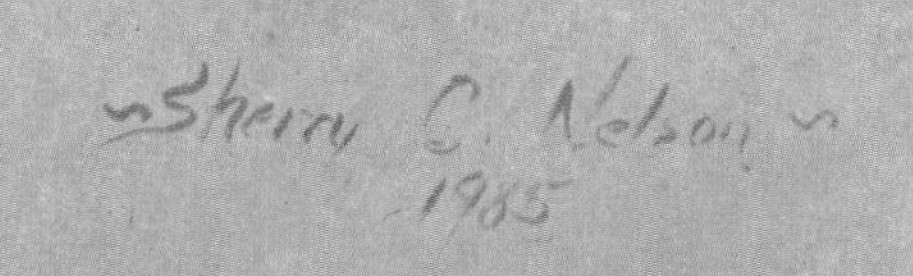

We have received many requests about Sherry's TV series, ''Birds—With A Magic Brush.'' This book presents the line drawings and painting instructions which Sherry teaches on the series. If you would like to see Sherry in your area with this excellent thirteen week series, contact your local PBS station and cable company and ask, ''When are you airing Sherry Nelson's thirteen week art instructional series, 'Birds—With A Magic Brush'?'' If you aren't receiving the series in your area, ask your station if they are planning on broadcasting it soon.

If you, or your local TV station, need more information about Sherry's series, or any of the other quality art instructional TV programs produced by *Decorative Arts Digest*, please write:

Decorative Arts Digest
90 W. Jersey Street
Orlando, FL 32806
Attn: Richard Truhn
or phone 305/841-7466

I hope you enjoy this book and our efforts to provide you with quality art instruction through TV broadcasting and our publications.

Sincerely,

Richard L. Truhn

Richard L. Truhn
Publisher
Decorative Arts Digest

Northern Oriole

Known in the East as the Baltimore Oriole and in the West as the Bullock's, the two birds comprise a single species: the Northern Oriole. The ranges of the two subspecies overlap on the Great Plains, and one or the other may be found throughout the United States. The female Northern Oriole is one of the most skillful builders of any bird, constructing a complex hanging nest of plant fiber, strings, and grass. Attached to a slender branch, the swaying sack-like construction is truly an incredible creation. This painting depicts the flashy male, an enjoyable addition to your collection of favorite bird paintings.

The 9″ × 12″ masonite background is painted with antique white acrylic which has been sprayed with matte finish and antiqued with splotches of RU oil paint. With the brush, apply oil paint, unthinned, and rub and buff into background panel with cheesecloth. When dry, respray and apply design.

The colors used are the following: Raw Umber, Burnt Umber, Ivory Black, Titanium White, Cadmium Orange and Cadmium Yellow Light. Use the following brushes: #8 bright and #1 round.

THE ORIOLE

Tail: Base / B + BU in the dark areas and with CO in the orange areas. Add feather lines with W in the dark areas and with B in the orange areas.

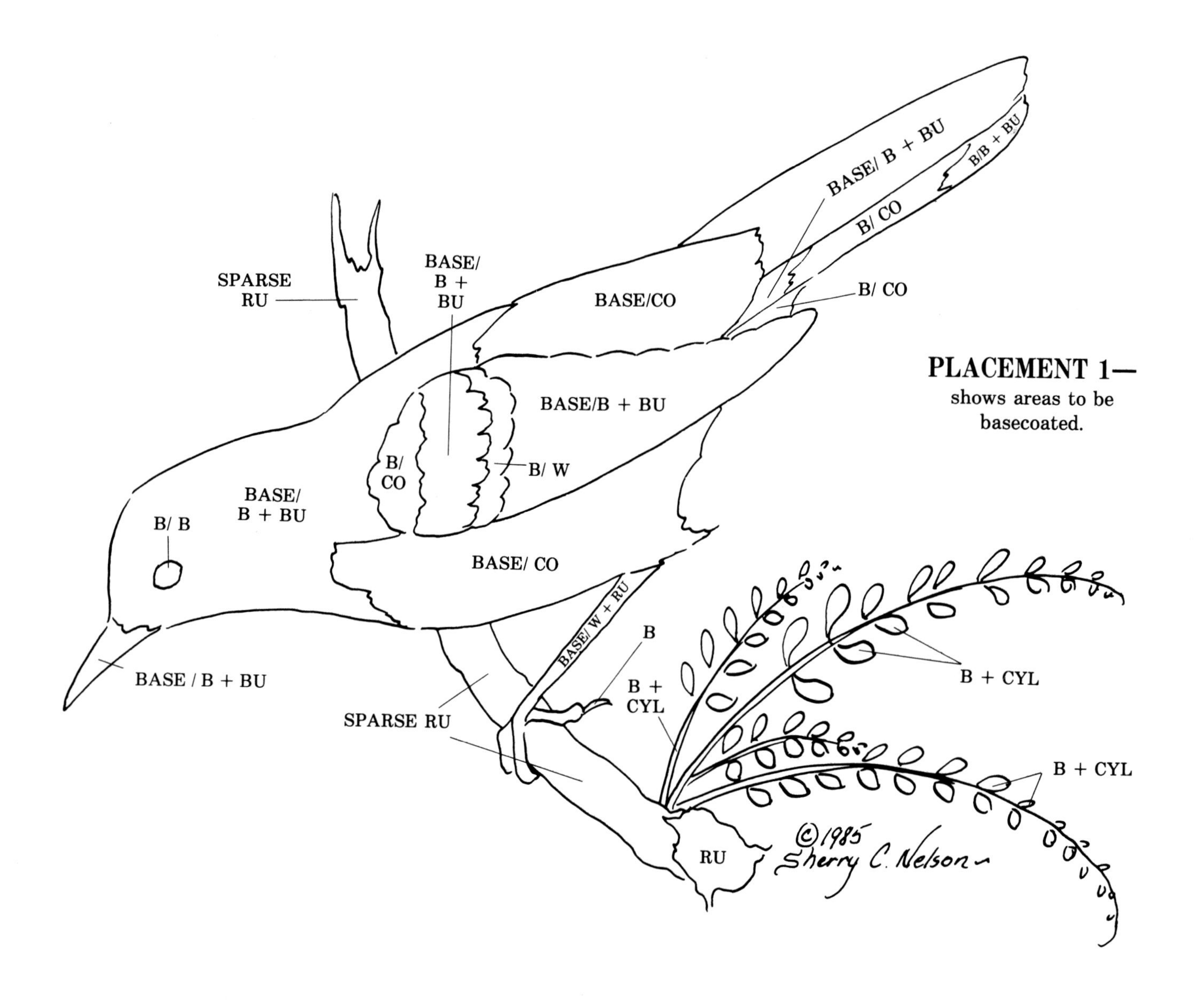

PLACEMENT 1— shows areas to be basecoated.

Bald Eagle

Instructions begin on page 61.

Red-headed Woodpecker

The Red-headed Woodpecker acquires his striking plumage during the first winter's molt, attaining the almost velvet-like red head and black-and-white 'tuxedo' by Spring. They are birds of the open woods, farmlands, parks, swampy areas and yards, searching tree trunks and ground for the insects, berries, and acorns that are their staple diet. Like the Eastern Bluebird, this woodpecker has diminished in numbers because of competition with Starlings for nesting cavities in dead trees and fence posts. Be a friend to a woodpecker: let that dead tree stand!

The background is a 9″ × 12″ masonite panel painted with light gray acrylic craft paint and sprayed with matte finish acrylic spray. The background has added interest by the application of RU, WG and W oils, applied in splotches and softly blended into background paint. When oils have dried, respray and apply design with artist's graphite.

The colors needed for this design are the following: Titanium White, Ivory Black, Raw Umber, Cadmium Yellow Light, and Bright Red. Brushes: #8 bright and #1 round.

THE WOODPECKER

Tail: Base / B. Streak in feather lines with W and chisel edge of brush.

Belly and Breast: Base / W. Shade where indicated with RU.

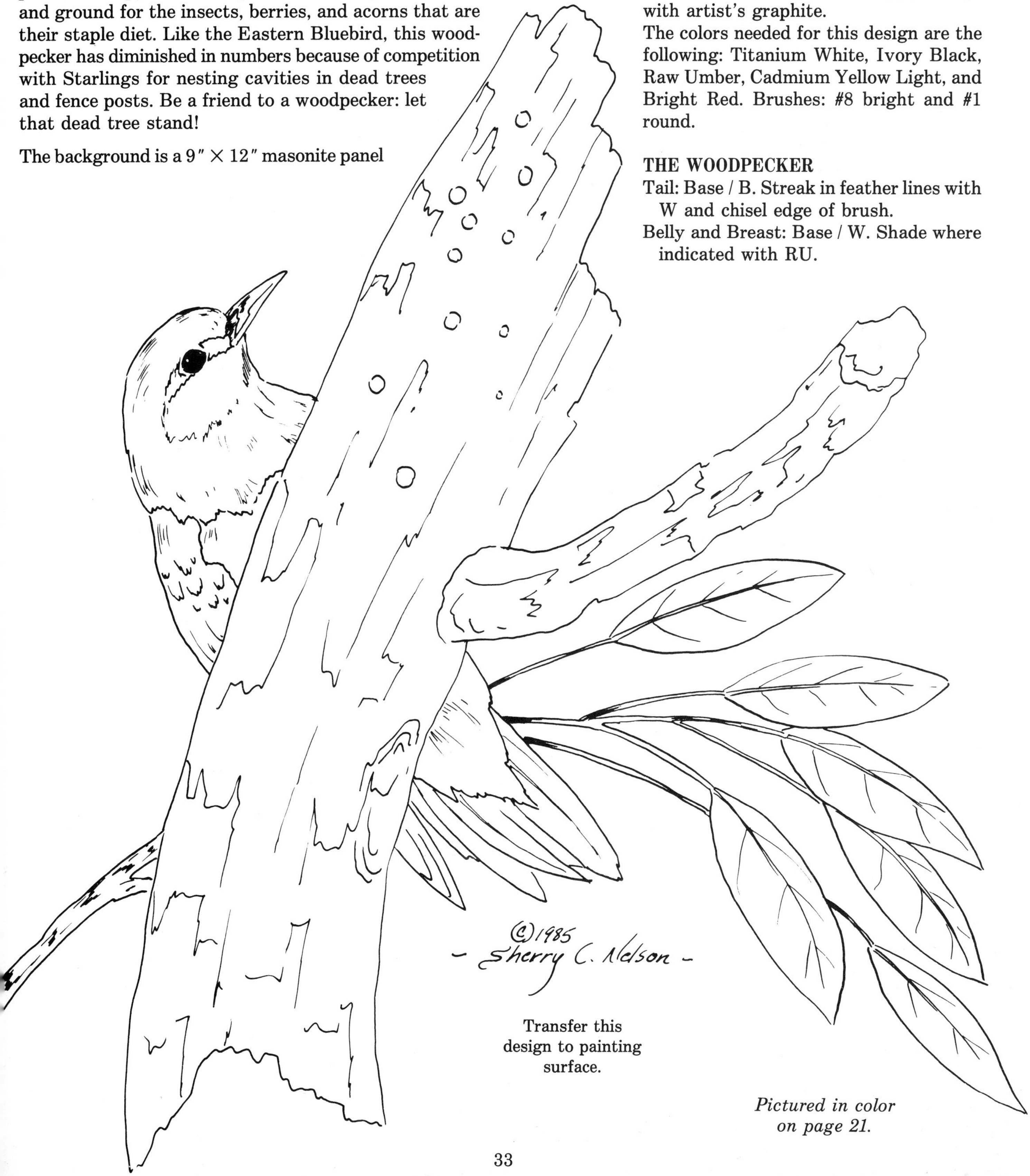

Transfer this design to painting surface.

Pictured in color on page 21.

Red-headed Woodpecker

Wing: Base / B. Apply feather lines with W, and detail soft markings on shoulder area with W.
Head: Base / BR. Shade where indicated with B. Highlight/ CYL + W.
Eye: Base / B. Highlight and outline with W.
Beak: Base / B. HL / W.

BRANCH

Lay on small amount of RU with brush. Rub into background with cheesecloth, establishing background color for detail. Then, where indicated on Placement 1, apply large shadow areas with slightly thinned RU. Chisel edges of shadow areas to indicate bark detailing. Add holes with B, using round brush, and make a tiny half circle of W inside the bottom edge of each one to give depth.

LEAVES

Apply B + CYL in dark areas shown on Placement 1. Pick up just a little turpentine with a mix of CYL + W and pull from edge of leaf to center as shown by arrows on placement 2. After growth direction has been set with light mixture, apply vein line to center of each leaf with the same light mix.

PLACEMENT 1

Indicates areas to be base-coated.

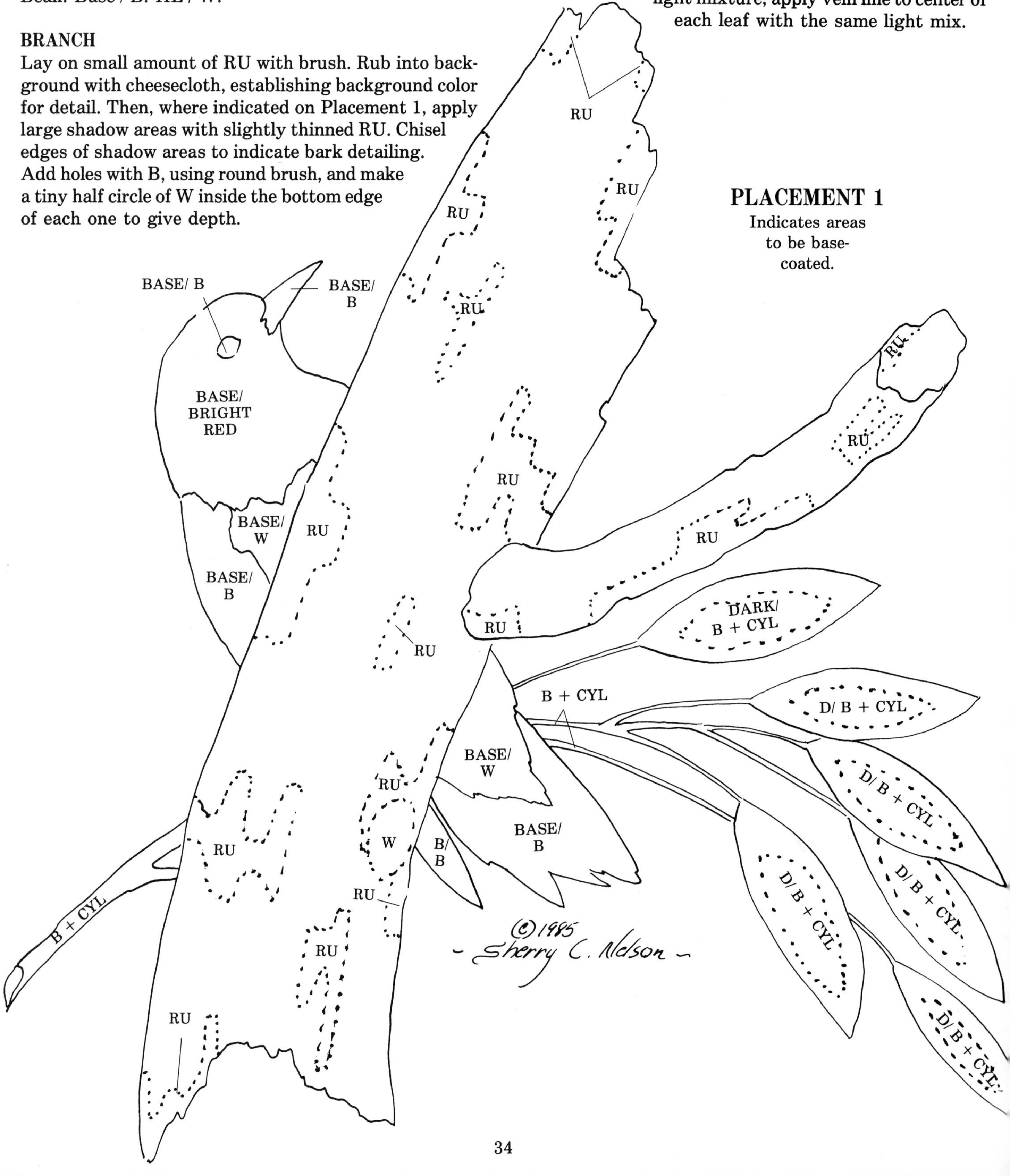

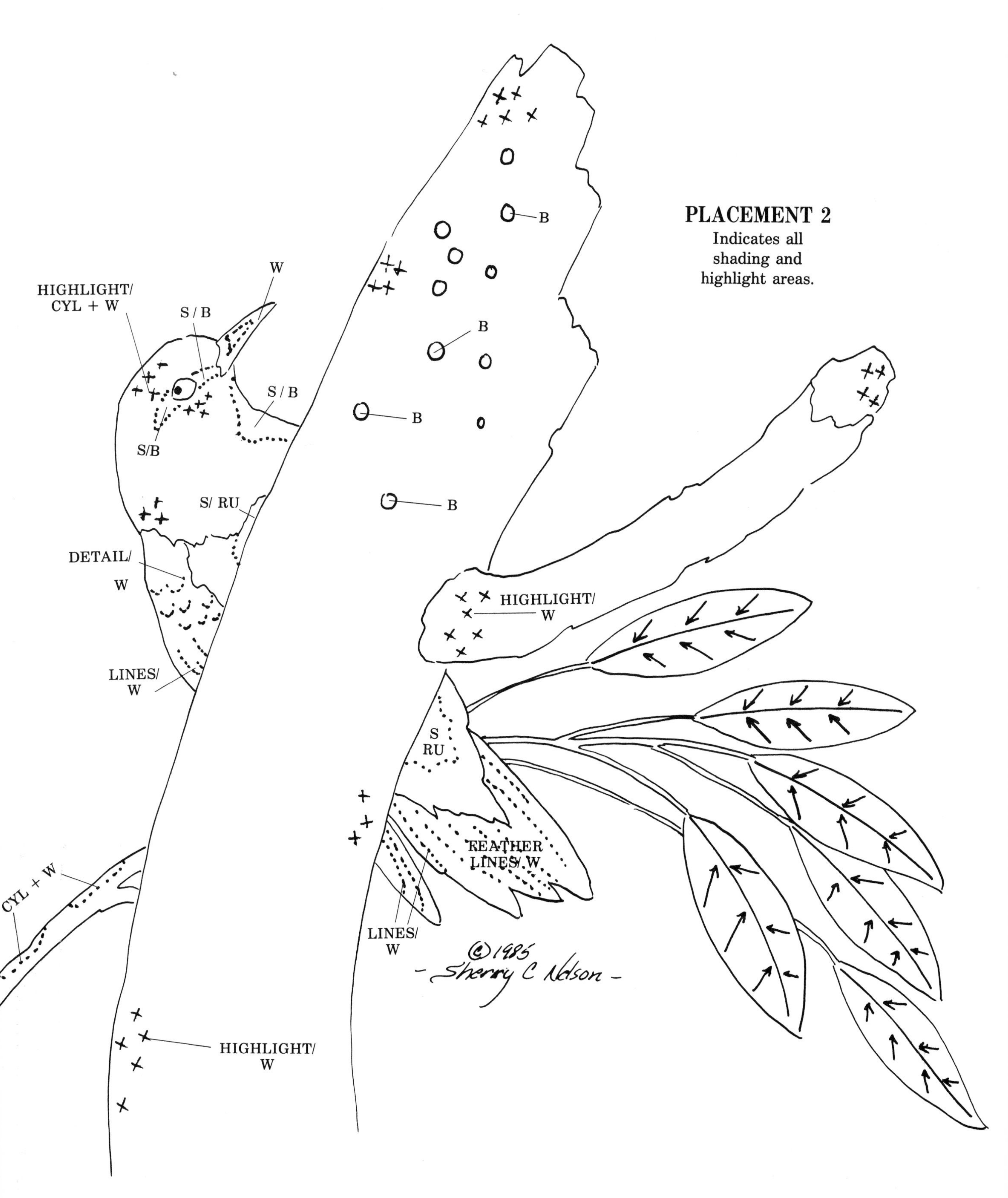
PLACEMENT 2
Indicates all shading and highlight areas.
W
HIGHLIGHT/ CYL + W
S / B
S / B
S/B
S/ RU
DETAIL/ W
LINES/ W
B
B
B
B
HIGHLIGHT/ W
S RU
FEATHER LINES/ W
LINES/ W
CYL + W
HIGHLIGHT/ W
©1985 - Sherry C Nelson -

The Common Loon

This extraordinary bird is perhaps best known for its loud, eerie nighttime cries, echoing across wilderness lakes in Canada and New England, as well as the Great Lakes region. You may well remember the beautiful scenes from the movie "Golden Pond" showing Loons in a natural setting, diving and swimming with power and grace. They can stay underwater for long periods of time, feeding—or diving as a means of escape. The Loon is a powerful flyer as well—and once in the air travels at speeds of up to 60 mph for long distances. But getting there is another matter—they require long stretches of open water along which they run and flap in order to get airborne!

(Continued on page 39)

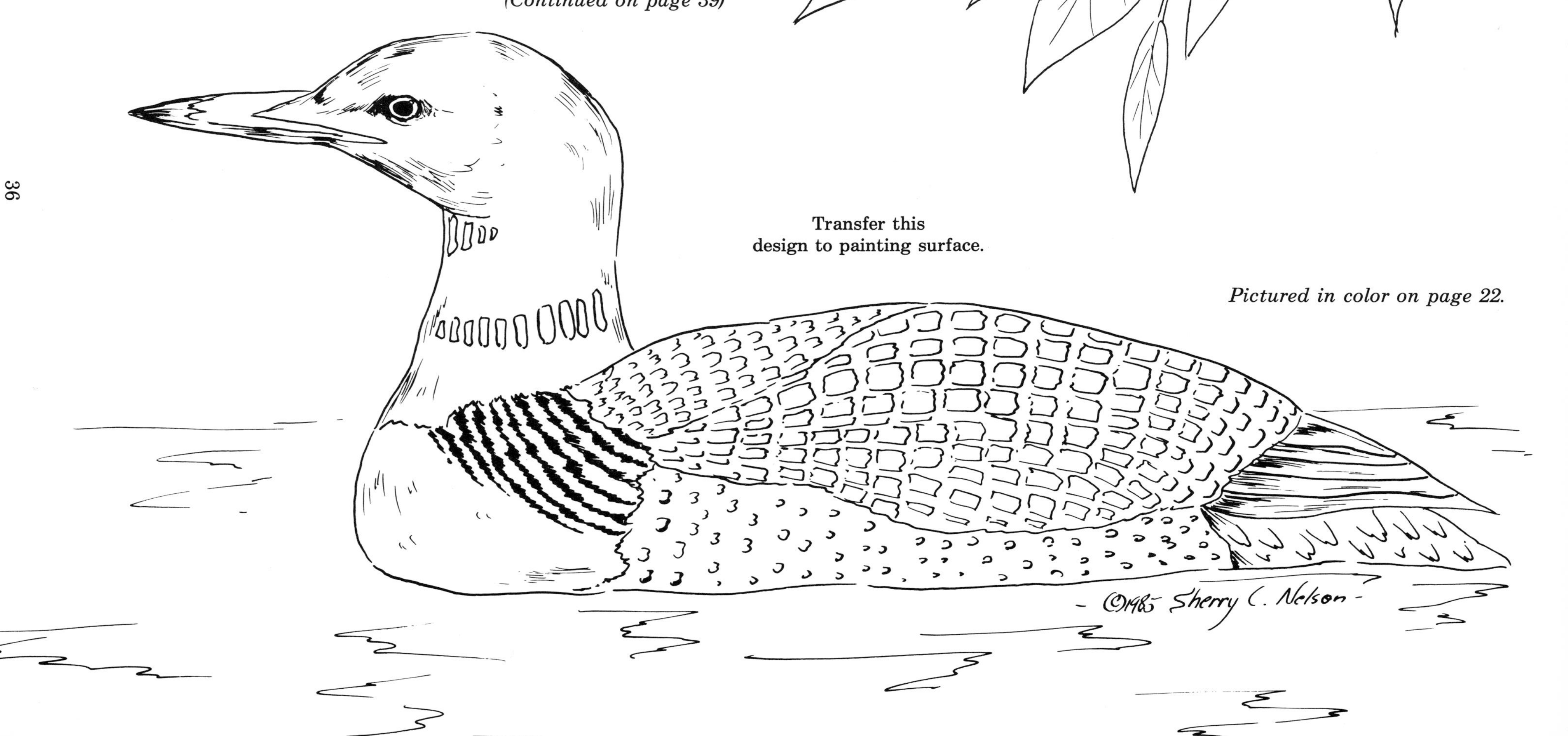

Transfer this
design to painting surface.

Pictured in color on page 22.

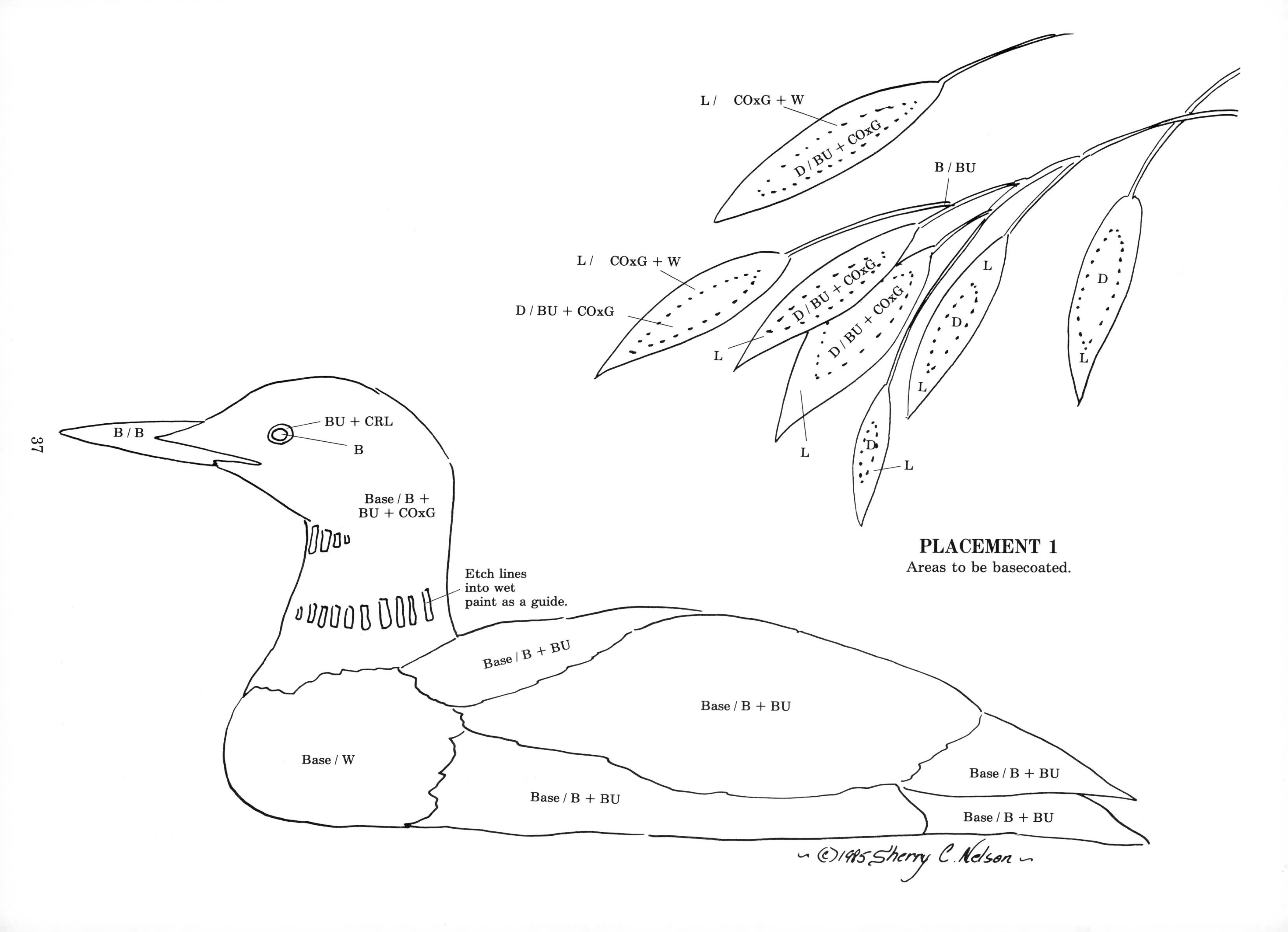
L / COxG + W
D / BU + COxG
B / BU
L / COxG + W
D / BU + COxG
D / BU + COxG
D / BU + COxG
L
L
D
L
D
L
D
L
L
B / B
BU + CRL
B
Base / B +
BU + COxG
Etch lines
into wet
paint as a guide.
PLACEMENT 1
Areas to be basecoated.
Base / B + BU
Base / B + BU
Base / W
Base / B + BU
Base / B + BU
Base / B + BU
©1985 Sherry C. Nelson

The Common Loon

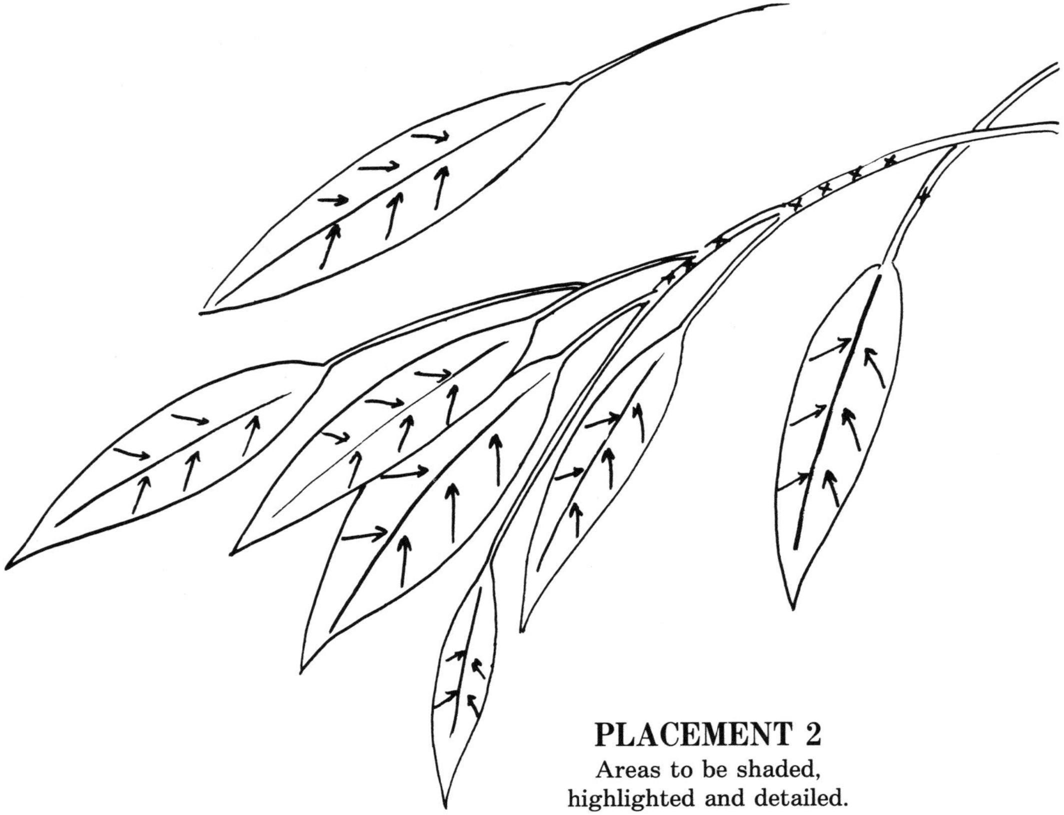

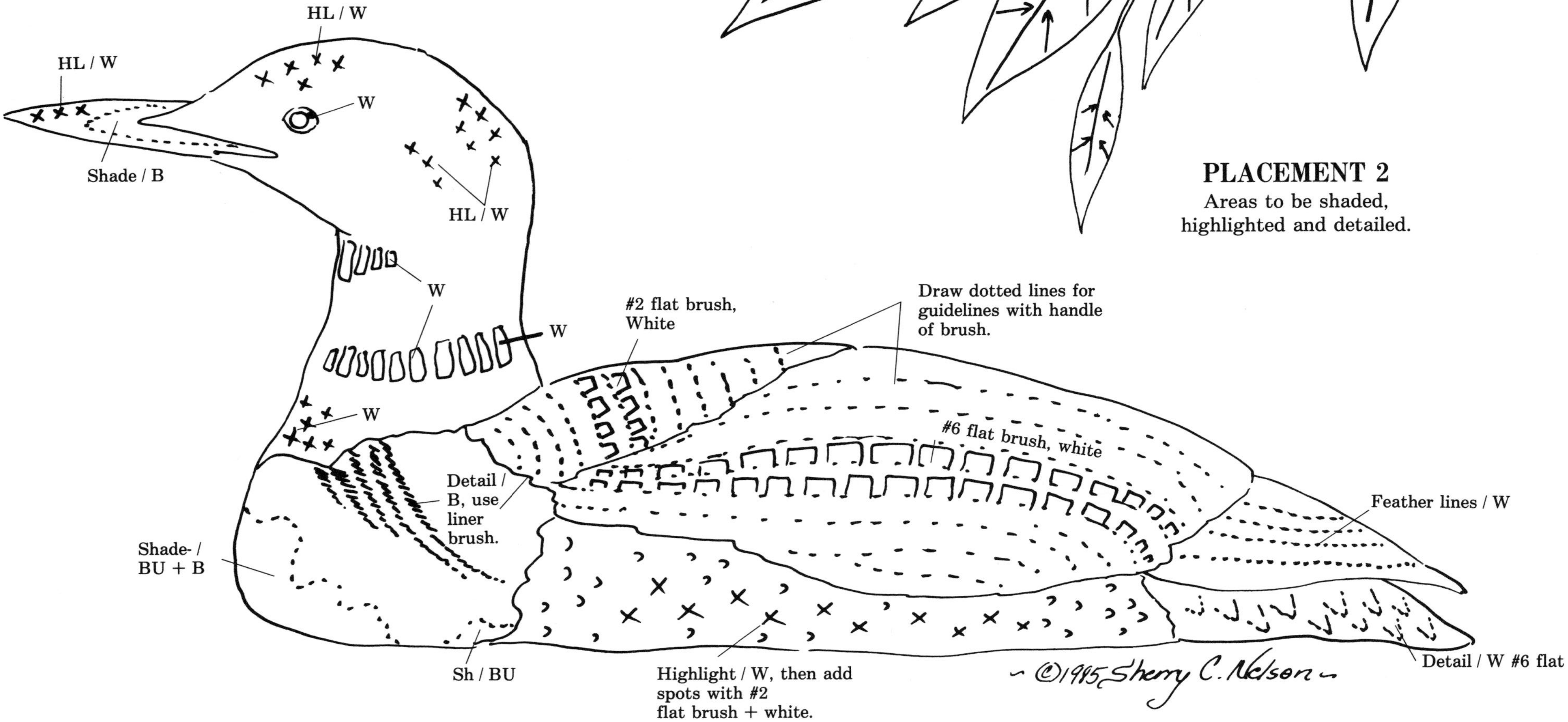

PLACEMENT 2
Areas to be shaded, highlighted and detailed.

HL / W

HL / W

W

Shade / B

HL / W

W

W

W

#2 flat brush, White

Draw dotted lines for guidelines with handle of brush.

#6 flat brush, white

Detail / B, use liner brush.

Feather lines / W

Shade- / BU + B

Sh / BU

Highlight / W, then add spots with #2 flat brush + white.

~ ©1995 Sherry C. Nelson ~

Detail / W #6 flat

The Common Loon

The background is a masonite panel size 9″ × 12″, painted with a light gray acrylic paint and sprayed with matte finish acrylic spray.

The colors used are the following: Ivory Black, Titanium White, Burnt Umber, Cadmium Red Light, and Chromium Oxide Green.

You will need a full range of brushes: #2 bright, #4 Bright, #6 Bright, #8 bright and a #1 round or pointed brush.

THE LOON

Tail: Base / B + BU. With #6 bright, loaded with W, pull detail markings as shown on Placement 2. Try using just the corner of the brush instead of applying it flat to the surface.

Primary wing feathers, above tail: Base / B + BU. Etch in feather lines with brush handle as you cover them with paint. Then place feather lines with W paint and chisel edge of #8 bright, sliding brush on chisel edge.

Side, next to water: Base / B + BU. Highlight W in area of xx's and blend into basecoat. Then add spotting with #2 bright and W paint where indicated on Placement 2.

Wing: Base / B + BU. As you block in base color and cover up the rows of feather markings, draw dotted lines with brush handle into wet paint for a guide. Start at front of section and draw slightly curved lines as shown on Placement 2. Then replace markings with #6 bright and W paint. Markings should be lightest, cleanest W at forward part of section and fade into background color at rear of section and at bottom of section.

Back: Base / B + BU. Add white markings as shown on Placement 2 with #2 or #4 bright. Smaller markings forward in section will do better with the #2 and the larger ones with the #4. Again, let the W fade out at rear of section.

Breast: Base / W. Shade with BU + B. Add B streaks with round brush and B paint as indicated.

Head and neck: Base / B + BU + just a little COxG. Etch neck and throat markings into wet paint with brush handle. Then replace them with W. Highlight dark head color with grayed white where indicated with xx's.

Eye: Base pupil B. Base iris CRL + BU. Highlight / W.

Beak: Base / BU + B + W. Shade / B. Highlight / W.

Reflections: Dark streaks / B + BU. Light streaks / dirty W. Pull color with #8 bright and rub out softly into background. Should be darkest next to bird.

LEAVES:

Dark area / BU+ COxG. Light area / COxG + W. Blend between dark and light areas after blocking the colors in. Then set a growth direction as indicated by arrows with a dry brush. Highlight some edges of leaves with W by pulling in same direction as for growth. They should appear quite smooth. After HL is applied, set in vein line with W paint and chisel edge of brush.

STEMS:

Base / BU. Highlight / W. Connect to leaf by pulling dark into top portion of leaf vein.

Eastern Bluebird

The Bluebird is a member of the Thrush family—and is the only one of its kind to nest in cavities in trees and fence posts. This bird of the orchard is so closely identified with its favored nesting site that I have chosen to include it as part of this design. In recent years the beautiful bluebird has declined because of competition from House Sparrows and Starlings for nest sites. Many bird enthusiasts came to the rescue with specially designed "bluebird" houses and a promising comeback has occurred. If you live in the Central or Eastern portions of the country, consider setting out some ready-made homes for these beautiful birds . . . your local Audubon Society can give you details on building them to suit.

The 9″ × 12″ masonite panel for this design is painted with off white acrylic and sprayed with a matte finish acrylic spray. To deepen and add interest behind the bird, I added WG and RU oil paint, rubbing it out into the background color with cheesecloth. When dry, respray and apply design with graphite paper.

The colors needed for this design are the following: Raw Sienna, Cadmium Red Light, Cadmium Yellow Light, Titanium White, Ivory Black, Raw Umber, Warm Gray and Ultramarine Blue.

You will need a #6 bright for the bird and a #8 bright for the fence post, as well as the #1 round for detail work.

THE BLUEBIRD

Tail: Base/ UB + WG. Pull a little W highlight from end of tail upward, and then add feather lines with W and chisel edge of brush. To make clean, sharp feather lines, hold flat brush the same position you would a pencil and slide chisel edge, the narrow edge of the brush, down the feather, forming a line of W highlighting.

Pictured in color on page 23.

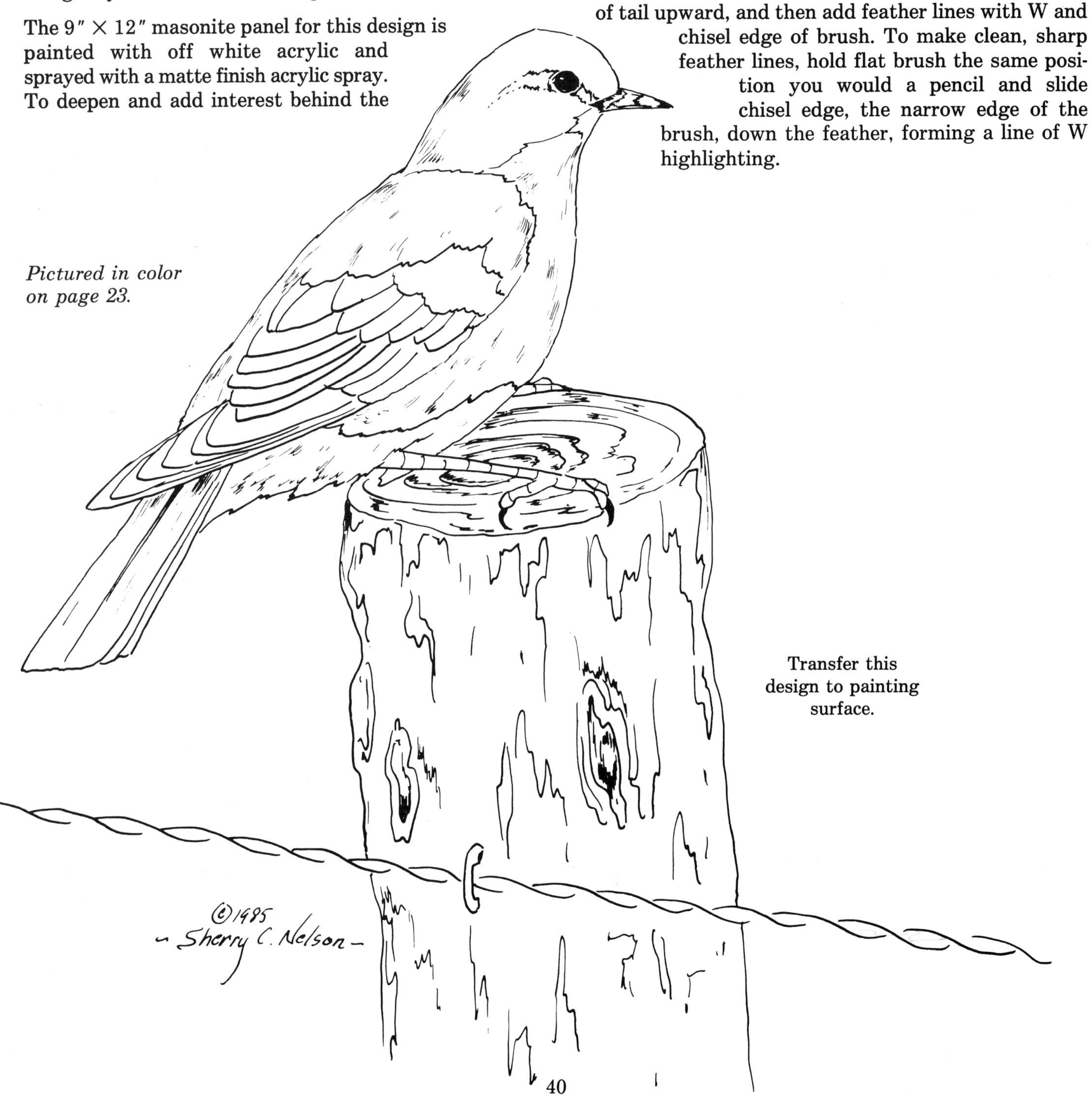

Transfer this design to painting surface.

Eastern Bluebird

Wing feathers: Base/ WG + UB. Add a little shading with B at the back portion of these feathers. As each graphite feather line is covered with paint, etch the line back into the wet paint with the wooden handle of the brush. When area is based and all feather lines are etched in, add the feather lines with W paint and chisel edge of brush, right on top of etched line.
Covert, top portion of wing: Base / WG + UB. Touch in feather texture with corner of flat brush and W.
Back, shoulder and head: Base / WG + UB. Highlight with W in areas of xx's. Blend slightly into basecoat color.
Belly and tiny spot under throat: Base / W. Shade with WG.
Breast: Base / RS + CRL. Use chisel edge of brush to edge these colors slightly into blue shoulder and neck colors. Do not blend them together. The HL breast area with CYL + W in area of xx's and blend slightly.
Eye, Beak and Legs: Base / B. Highlight / W. Add segment lines on leg with B, using round brush.

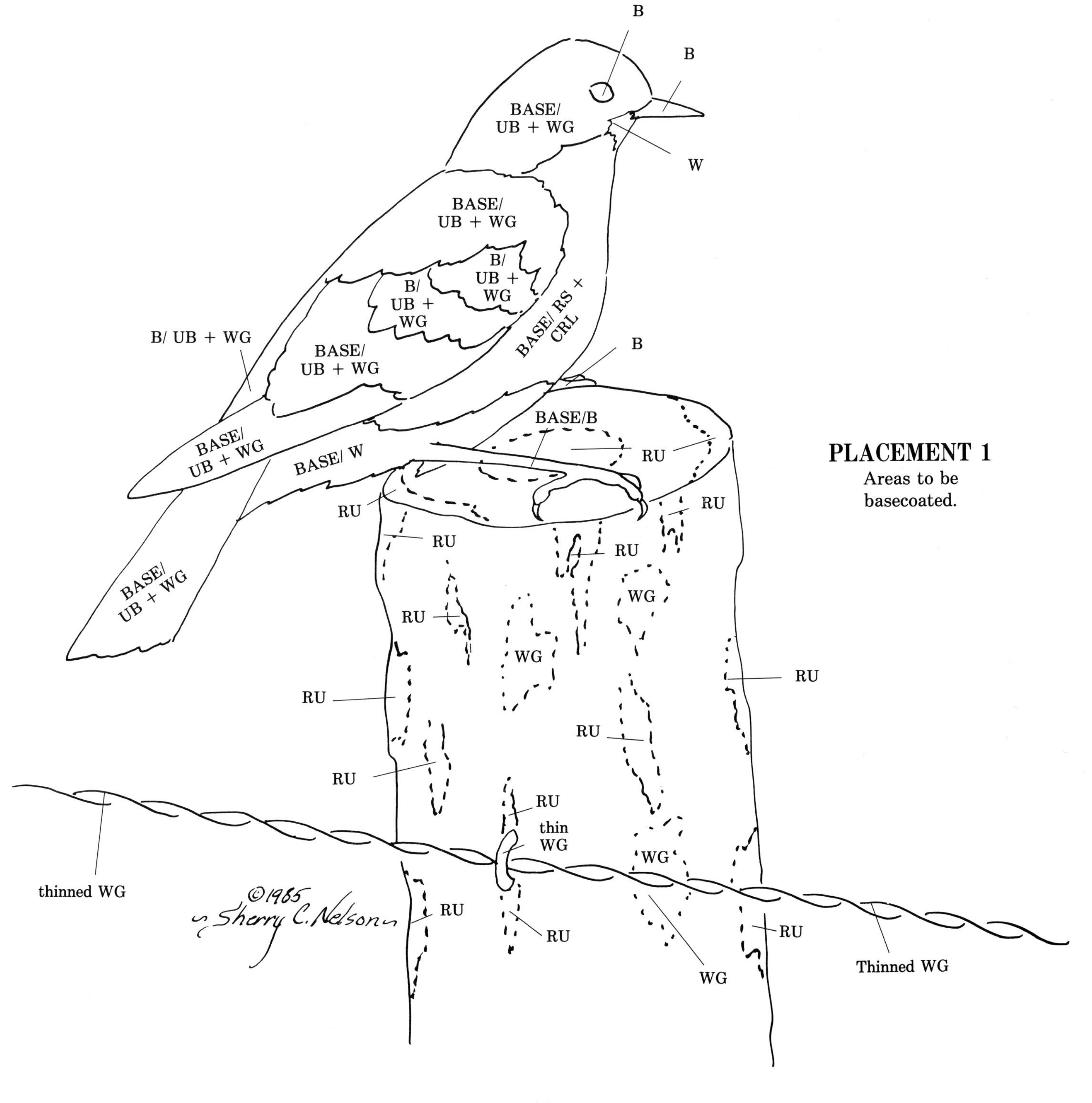

POST:
Chisel in area of RU as shown. Add some areas of WG. Rub out with finger or cheesecloth. Then detail with thinned RU on round brush as shown on placement 2.

WIRE:
Base with thin WG. Add curving detail lines with thinned B on round brush.

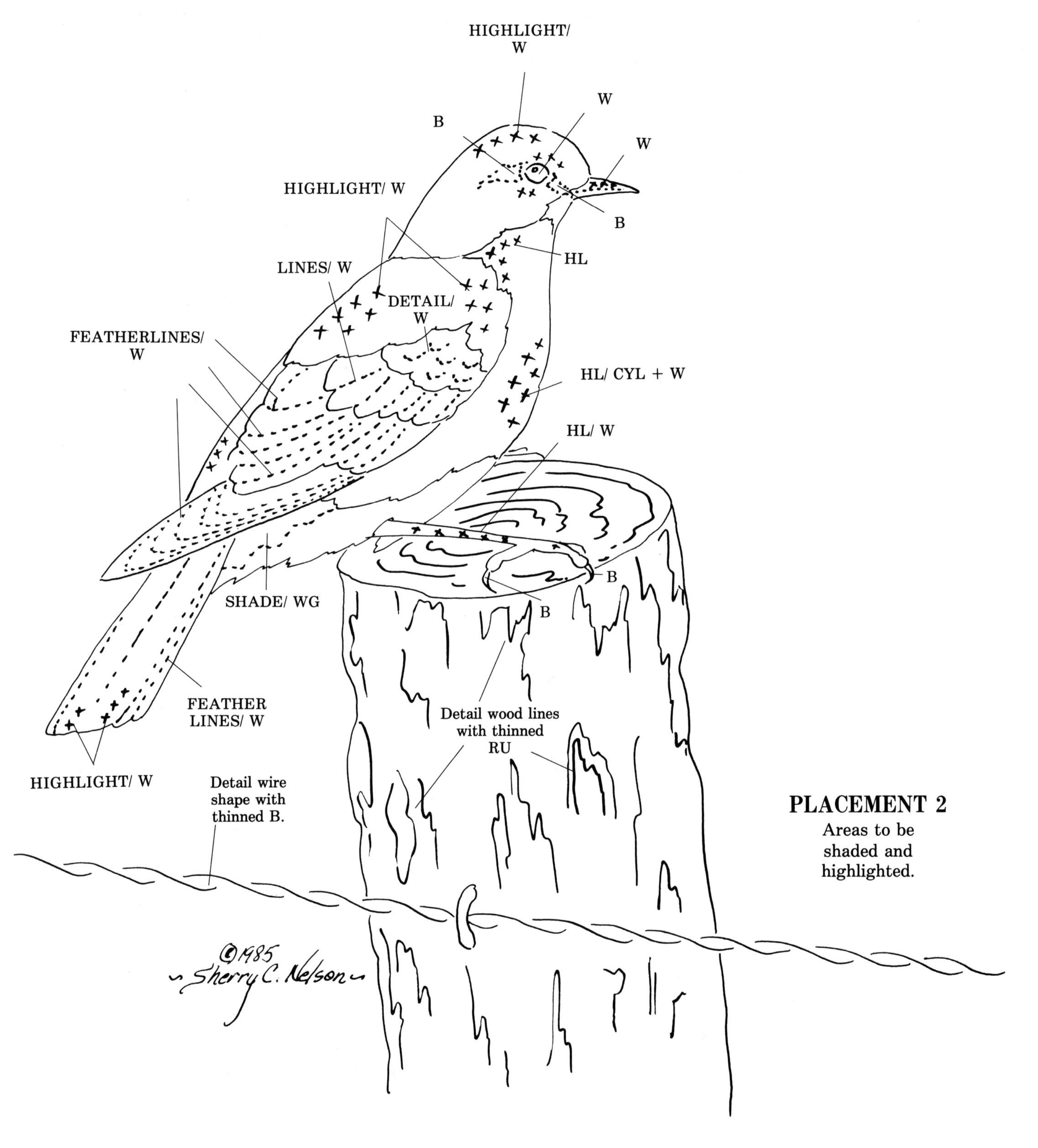

PLACEMENT 2
Areas to be shaded and highlighted.

The Mallard

The most widely-recognized and well-known duck in the United States, the Mallard is also the most numerous. Found in the most remote areas—as well as in city parks and on farm ponds, the Mallard drake makes a striking and exciting painting subject. A favorite game bird as well, the "puddle duck" feeds by tipping tail up to reach water plants and seeds. When startled, this agile bird can take off almost vertically from the water, providing a show that's beyond compare!

The background panel is 11"×14" masonite, painted with antique white acrylic paint and sprayed with matte finish acrylic spray.

The colors needed are Cadmium Yellow Medium, Burnt Sienna, Ultramarine Blue, Chromium Oxide Green, Raw Umber, Burnt Umber, Ivory Black, Titanium White, Yellow Ochre and Raw Sienna. A #8 bright and a #1 round brush is also needed.

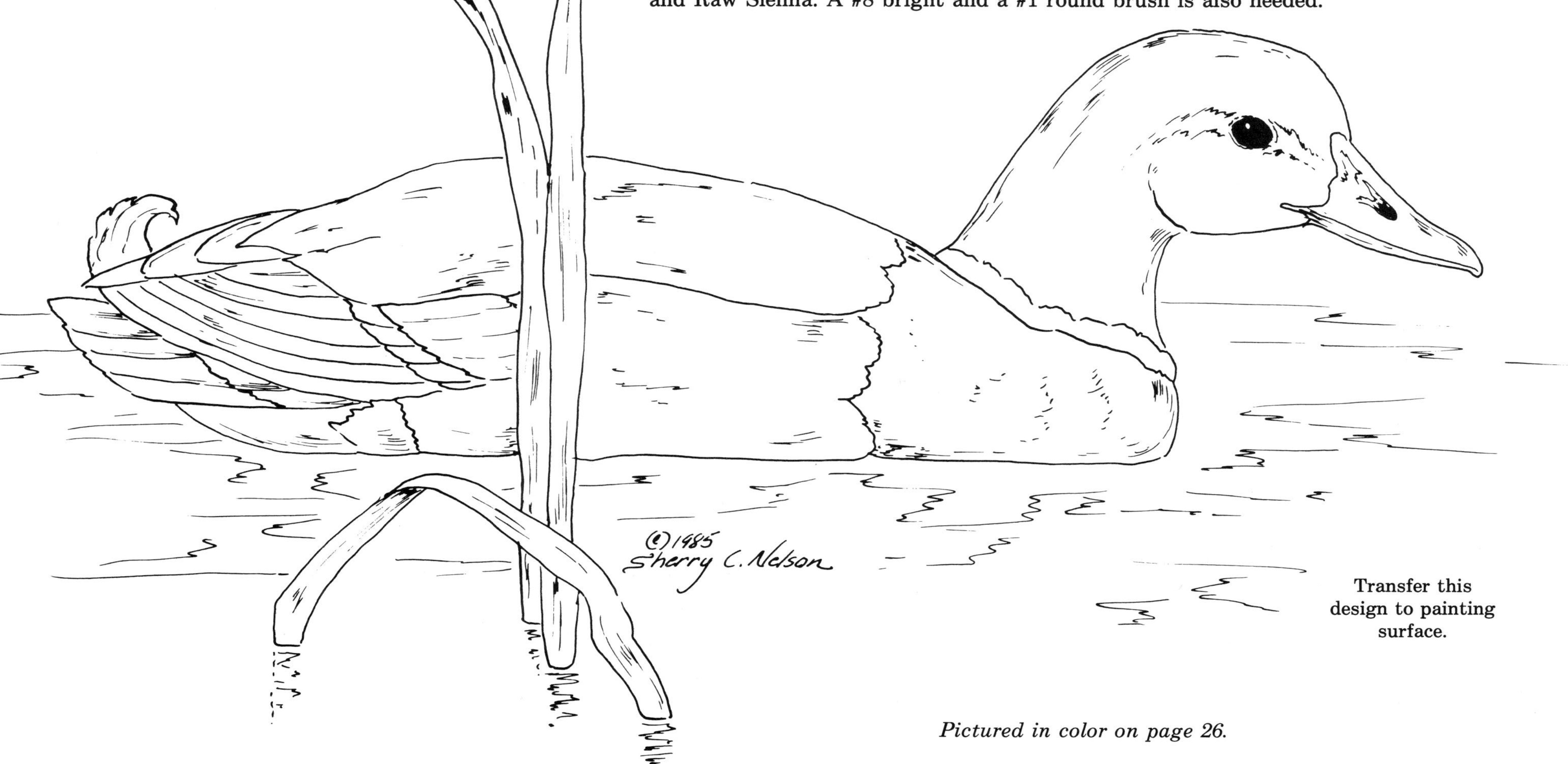

Transfer this design to painting surface.

Pictured in color on page 26.

The Mallard

THE MALLARD

Drake feathers, curling up from tail: Base / B. Highlight / W.

Tail: Base outer portion with W, inner portion with B. Blend with chisel edge of brush in direction of arrows and add feather lines with B on chisel edge of brush.

Undertail Coverts: Base / B.

Flank patch, to right of covert area: Base / W.

Primary flight feathers: Base / BU. Etch feather lines into wet paint with brush handle. Then paint feather lines with W.

Speculum, the blue and white patch: White feathers, B / W. Blue feather, B / UB + RU. Highlight blue area with a little W. Edge blue area into white band to connect and then add feather lines in W area with RU.

Back: Base / W + just a little RU. Shade with RU where indicated. Blend in direction of growth of feathers.

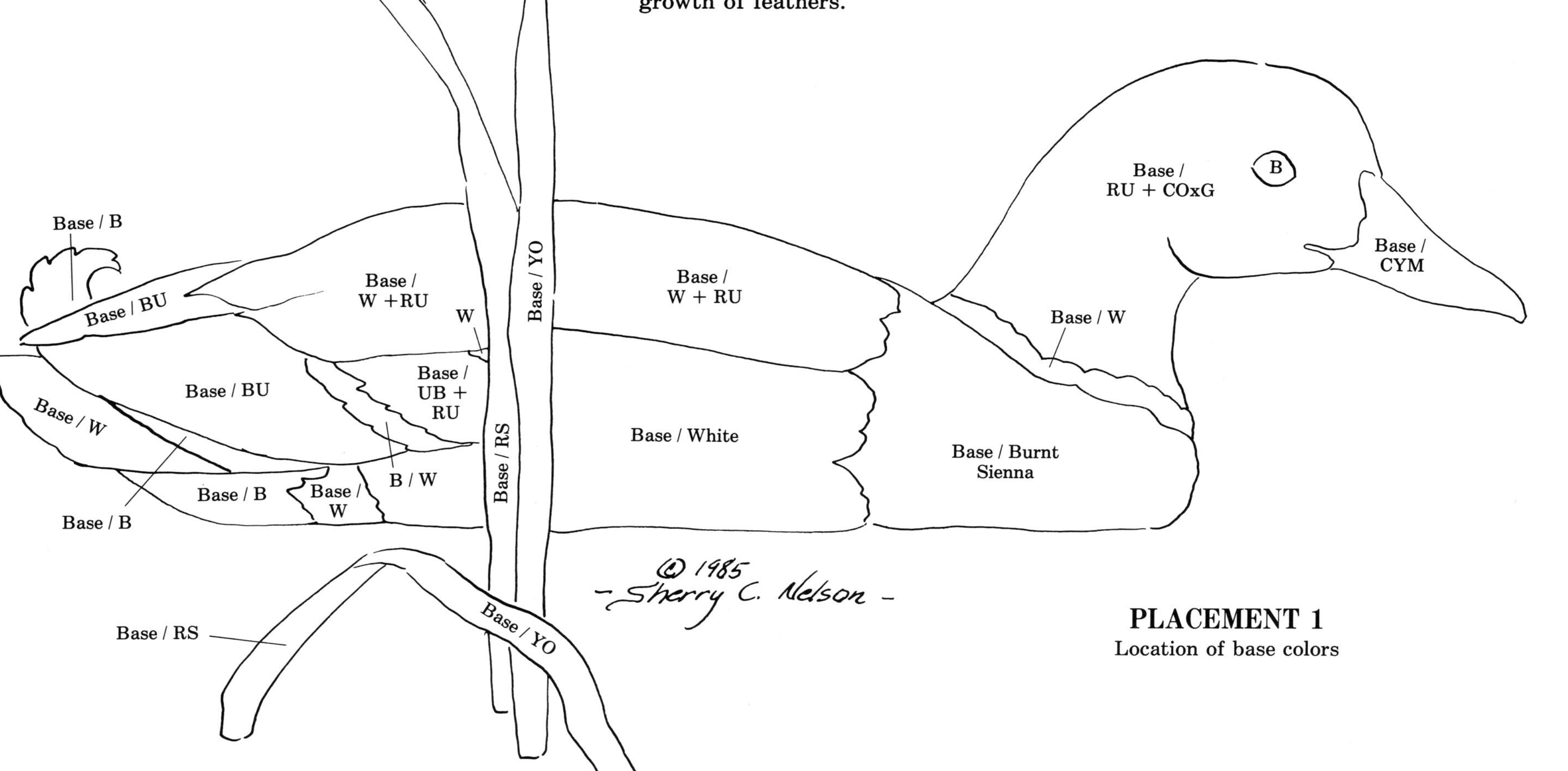

PLACEMENT 1
Location of base colors

Side: Base / W. Shade with RU where shown on placement 2.
Breast: Base / BS. Shade with BU. Highlight with dirty W so that highlight is not too bright.
Neck band: Base / W. Shade / RU.
Head: Base / RU + COxG. This mixture should still look *green* but not too intense. Shade where shown on placement 2 with RU and B. Highlight in area of xx's with CYM + W. If needed, additional highlight may be added with W.
Eye: Base / B. HL / W.
Bill: Base / CYM. Shade / RS. Nostril area / RS. HL / W.

REEDS:
Back reed: Base / RS. Forward Reeds: Base / YO. HL all reeds with CYM + W.

REFLECTIONS:
Using the same basecoat colors as for the duck, streak and rub some color directly below each area, darkening closer to the duck and fading farther out into the water. Reflection color for reeds is RU. Cut back into reflection colors with brush dampened with turpentine, lifting out some of the color for a rippled look.

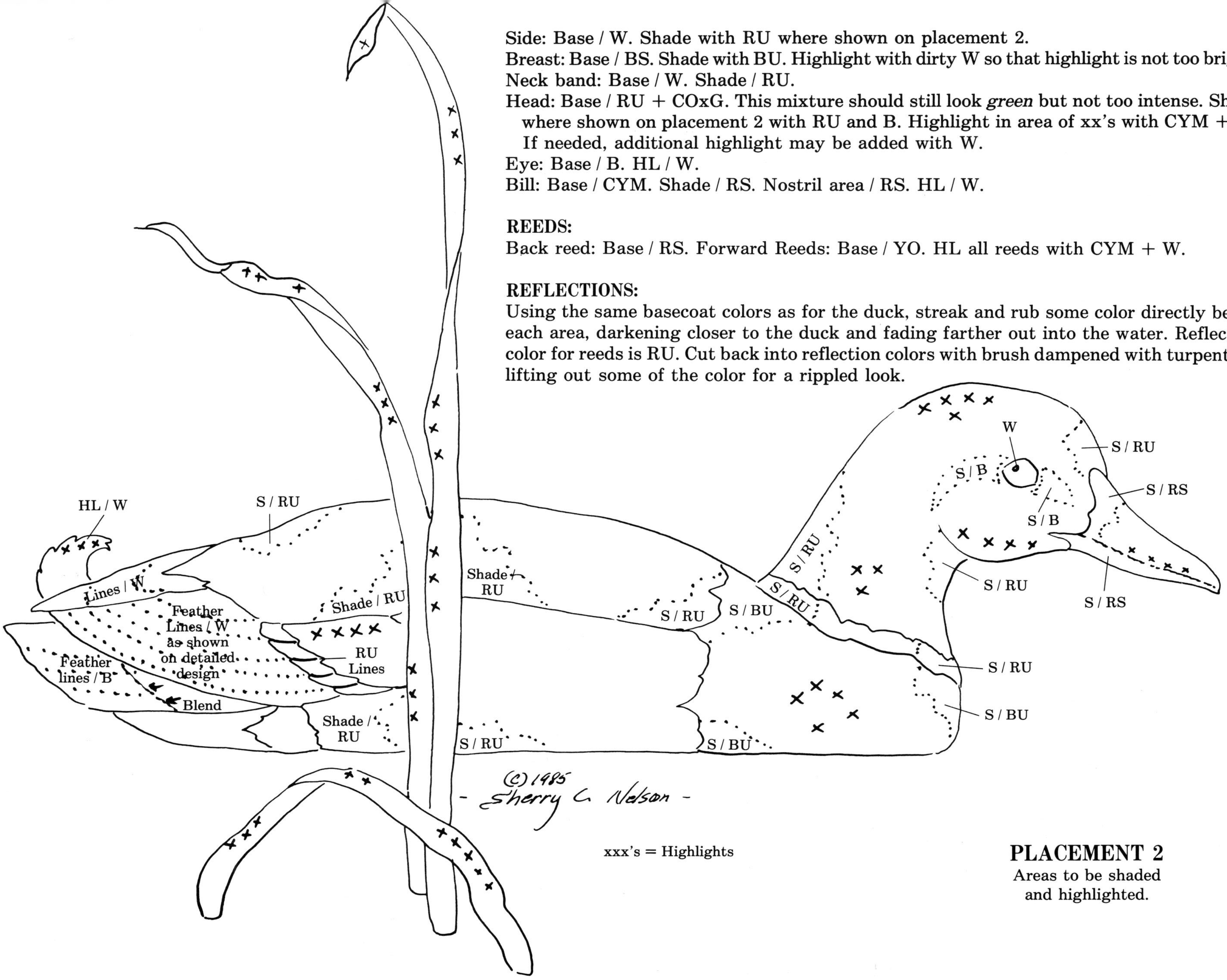

PLACEMENT 2
Areas to be shaded
and highlighted.

American Robin

Robin-Redbreast-harbinger of Spring! Probably the Robin is known more widely throughout the United States than any other bird . . . A summer or winter resident in every single state except Hawaii, it brights up both suburb and remote forest with its variable, cheerful song. Have a friend or acquaintance in need of a lift? Paint them a Robin and spread a little cheer!

This design is painted on a masonite panel, size 9″×12″, painted with antique white acrylic and sprayed with a matte finish acrylic spray.

The colors used are these: Warm Gray, Ivory Black, Titanium White, Raw Sienna, Raw Umber, Burnt Umber, Cadmium Red Light, Cadmium Yellow Light, and Burnt Sienna.

You will need a #8 bright and a #1 round red sable brush.

THE ROBIN

Tail: Base / WG + BU. Add feather streaks and lines with W and chisel edge of flat brush.

Back: Base / WG. HL where indicated on placement 2 with W. Blend just a little between colors.

Primary wing feathers: Base / BU. As feather lines are covered with paint, etch them into wet paint with handle of brush. Then paint in lines with chisel edge of brush and W paint.

Pictured in color on page 27.

Secondaries: Base / RU. Again etch in feather lines for a guide, then paint them with W.

Upper wing: Base / RU. With corner of flat brush and a dry load of W, pull on feather markings as indicated. They should not be distinct nor defined.

Belly: Base / W. Shade / WG.

Breast: Base / BS + CRL. Highlight first with CYL + W, then with straight W. HL areas are indicated on placement 2 and should be blended just a little into the basecoat color.

Head: Base / B + BU. Highlight just a little with W.

Eye: Base / B. Highlight / W. Add markings, as on design around eye with round brush and W paint. Add chin streaks with chisel edge of flat brush and W paint. Do not blend these areas; just apply color.

Beak: Base / RS + CYL. Shade at top portion with BS. Shade at tip of beak with RU. Highlight in area of xx's with CYL + W.

Legs: Base / RS. Shade upper portion with RU. Streak a bit of HL down center of shaft of leg with W. Then add detail lines with B as shown on inked design.

GRASSES

Fill in blades of grass quickly and without undue detail, using CYL + B. It will be more attractive if you achieve several values of green for interest. When grass is dry, rub in RU underneath grassy area with flat brush, and blend lightly into background with cheesecloth to indicate a ground area.

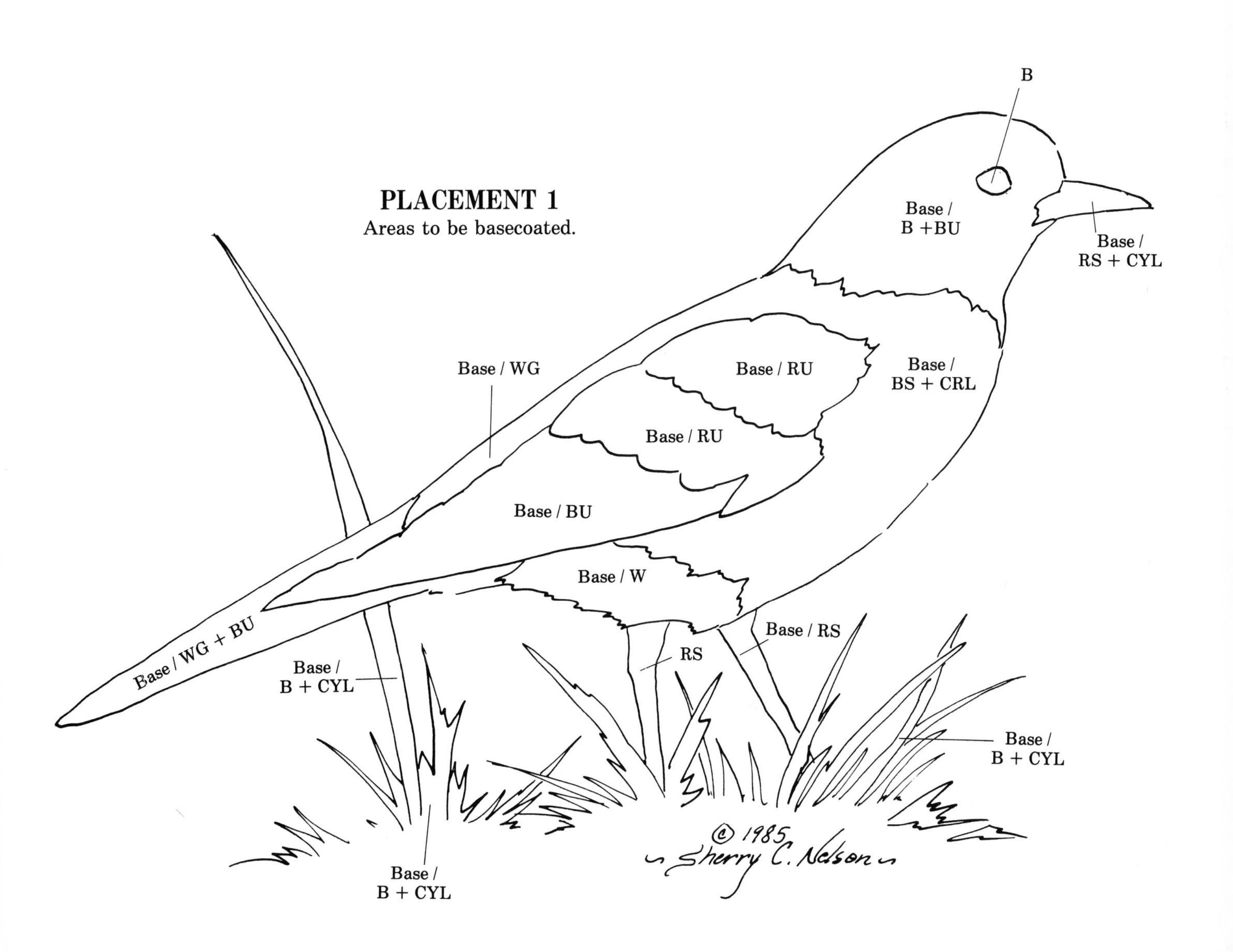

American Robin

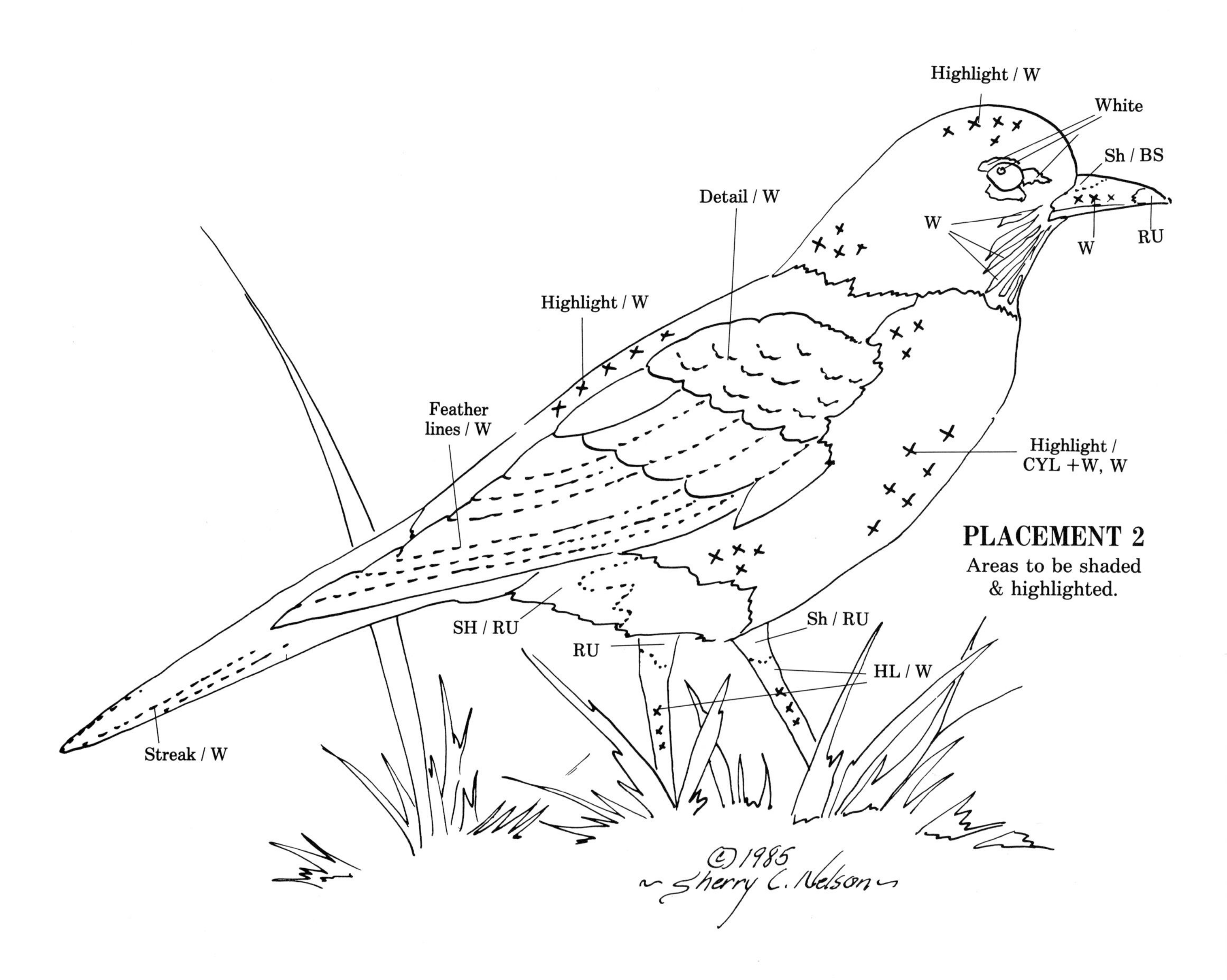

The Northern Cardinal

The beautiful scarlet Cardinal has been chosen as the state bird by seven states, more than any other bird—attesting to its great popularity throughout the country. It has become a symbol of the winter holiday season, bringing Christmas cheer on cards and in decorations. The brilliant red against the garlands of green cannot help-but-make-this-one-of-your-favorite-birds!

The background is a 9″×12″ masonite panel painted with light gray and sprayed with matte finish acrylic spray. The oil colors used to attain the mottled, out-of-focus setting for the bird were RU + COxG and W. Rub the dark mix into the background first— then the W.
When dry, respray and apply design with Artist's graphite paper.

Colors needed are the following: Raw Umber, Permanent Green, Titanium White, Ivory Black, Winsor Orange, Bright Red, Mars Brown, Burnt Umber, and Cadmium Scarlet. Use a #6 bright, a #8 bright and a #1 round.

THE CARDINAL

Tail: Base / BR + MB. Shade with BU at base of Tail. Add feather lines with WO + W.

Wing feathers: Base / BR + MB + BU. Etch feather lines into wet paint with wooden handle of brush to use as a placement guide for the light mix. Then add feather lines with mixture of WO + W as shown on placement 2.

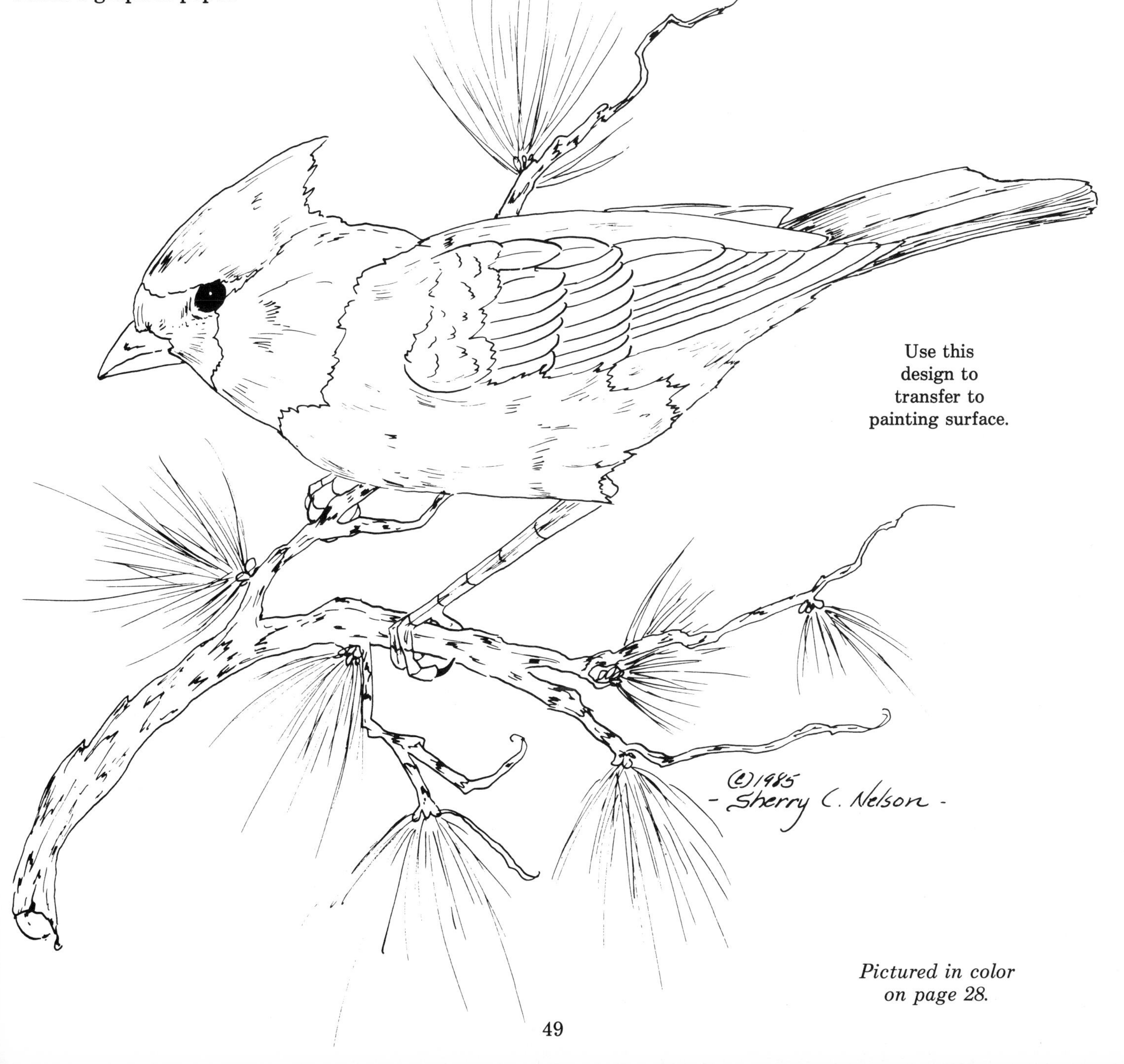

Use this design to transfer to painting surface.

Pictured in color on page 28.

The Northern Cardinal

Shoulder: Base / MB + BR. Add tiny feather markings with WO + W, just to texture.
Back: B / MB + BU. Highlight with a dirty brush + W paint.
Undertail coverts: Base / BU + MB.
Breast: Base / BR. Blend this color into shoulder of wing, back and undertail feathers with chisel edge of brush. Highlight in all areas indicated with xx's using the chisel edge of brush and WO + W. Using the chisel edge will help achieve some texture within this area.
Head, red portions: Base / CS + BR.
Shade with a little MB where shown and blend into other color. Highlight, again striving for a little texture, with WO + W.
Head, black portion: Base / B. Cut into red with corner of brush. Do not blend into red.
Eye: Base / B. Highlight / W.
Beak: Base / BR. HL / WO + W.
Leg: Base / BU. Streak shaft of leg with a little BR + MB to redden. HL / dirty W. Add detail segment lines and claws with B.

BRANCH:
Apply dark with RU and light with W. Chop together to achieve bark-like texture.

NEEDLES:
Thin a mixture of PG + RU and use round brush to apply needles. If strokes are too heavy, add a little more turpentine to mix and try again, holding brush vertical to surface. Add W needles if desired for added interest.

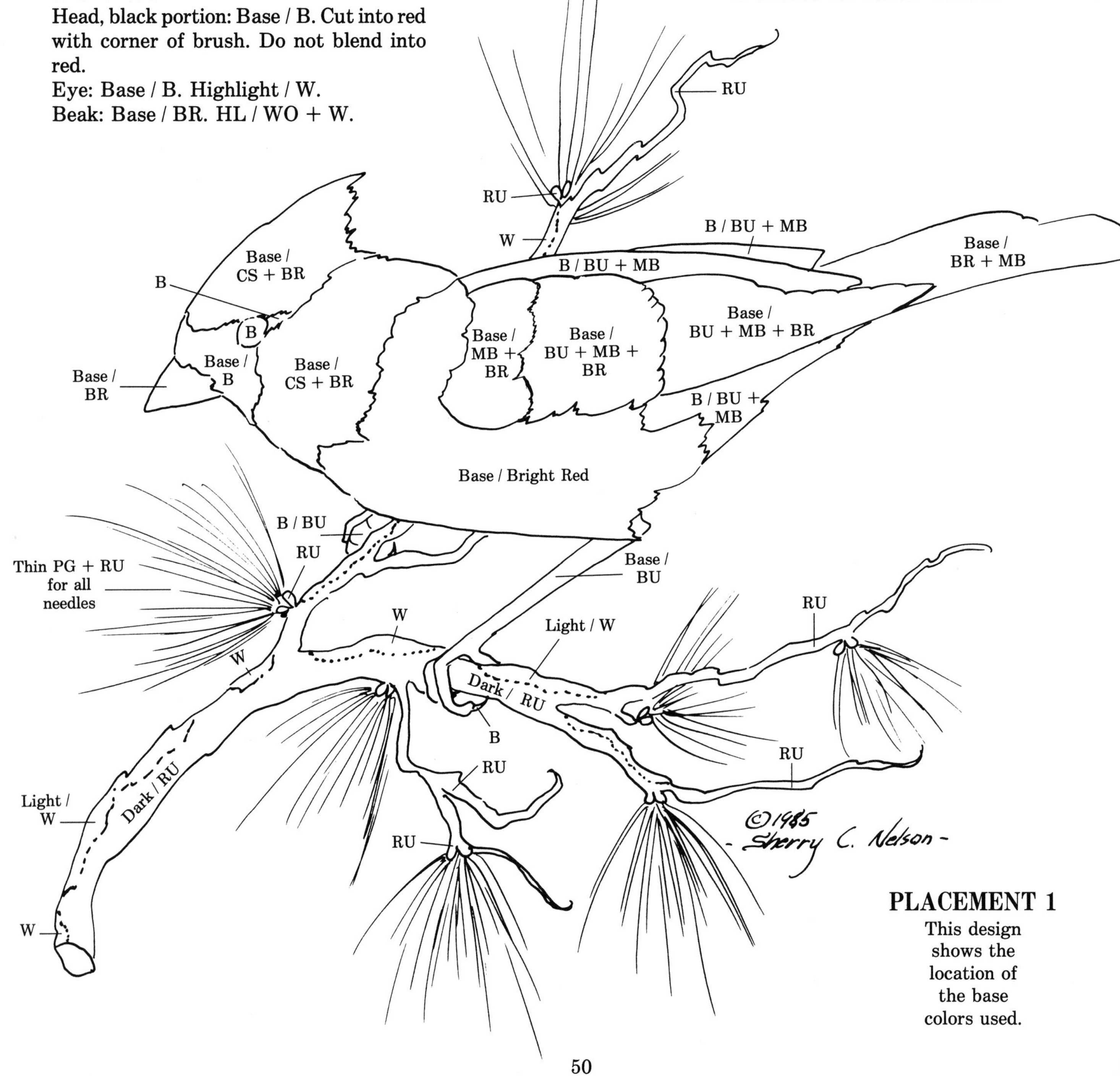

PLACEMENT 1
This design shows the location of the base colors used.

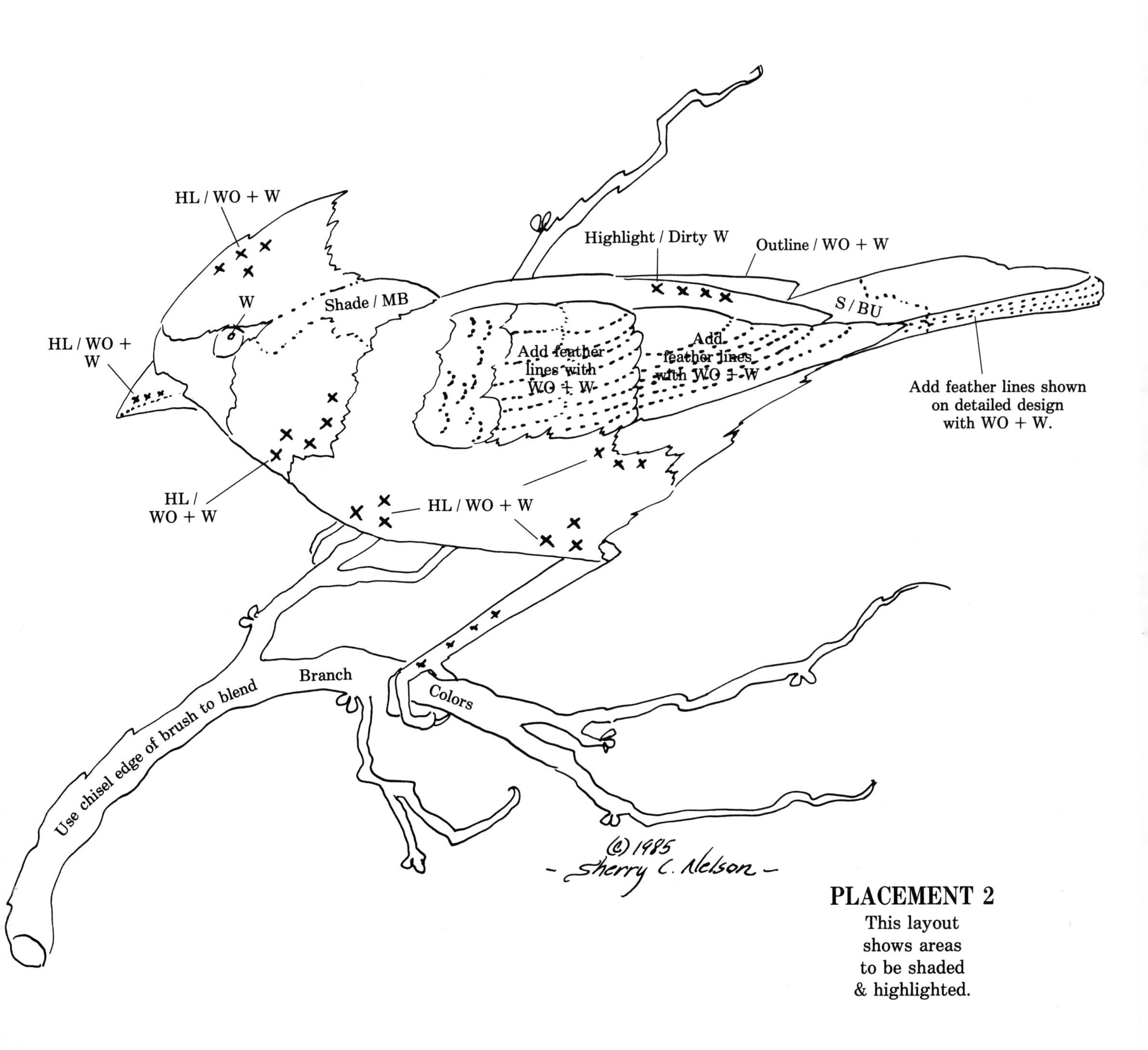

PLACEMENT 2

This layout shows areas to be shaded & highlighted.

The Canada Goose

Pictured in color on page 29.

Pictured in color on page 29.

Transfer this
design to
painting surface.

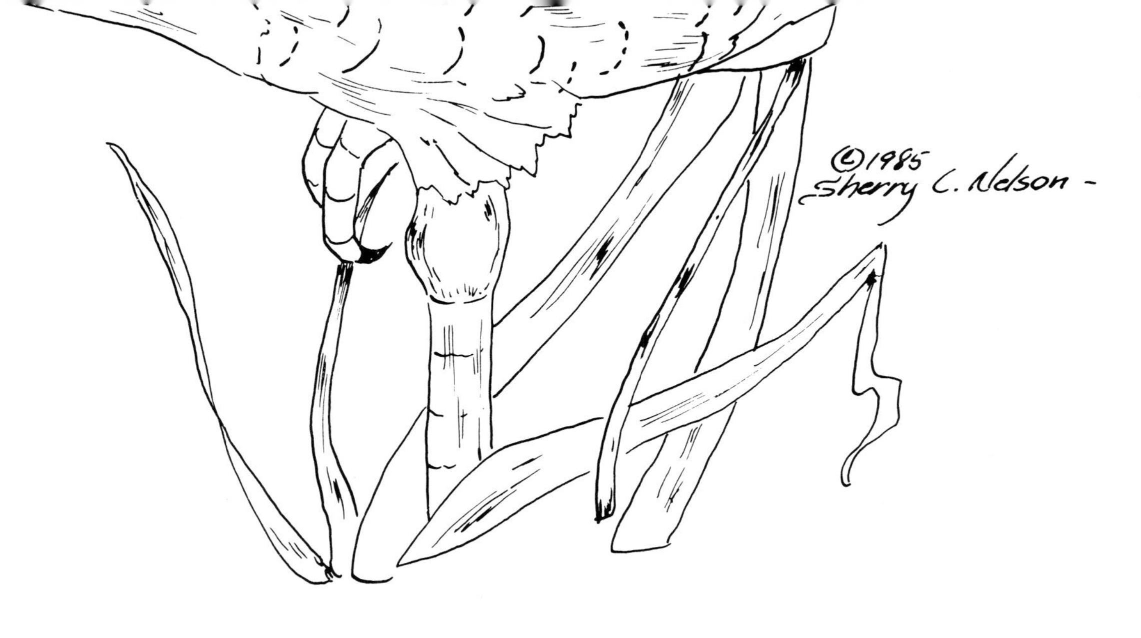

The most widespread and common of the wild geese in American, the Canada Goose makes a wonderful painting subject. With the distinctive white throat patch and black 'stocking' neck, this beautiful goose would make the perfect painting to give to a hard-to-please friend—or to hang in den or living area.

The background color, a gray-blue, is rolled on the 11″×14″ masonite panel, and sprayed with matte finish acrylic. The out-of-focus effect is achieved with RU, WG and W. When background colors are dry, respray and transfer design with Artist's graphite paper.

The oil colors used in this design are the following: Ivory Black, Titanium White, Cadmium Yellow Light, Van Dyke Brown and Burnt Sienna.

Brushes needed will be #8 bright and #1 round.

THE CANADA GOOSE

Tail: Base / B. Add feather lines as indicated on Placement 2 with W, using chisel edge of flat brush.

Undertail Feathers: Base / W. Shade where indicated with VDB.

Primaries, left of tail: Base with VDB as shown. As each feather line is covered with paint, etch back in with wooden handle of brush to use as a placement guide for light feather lines. Use chisel edge of brush and W for feather lines.

Back feathers, left of primaries: Base in alternate bands of W and VDB. After entire area is based, blend with chisel edge of brush in direction of arrows on Placement 2. Effect should be quite soft, with W edges very dull.

Belly: Base / VDB + W, a fairly dark mixture. Then highlight with W over basecoat by pulling strokes in direction of arrows.

Breast: Base W. Shade where indicated with VDB. Then blend right edge of this section into back and belly feathers using a choppy motion of brush for texture. Highlight center area of breast with W as shown by xx's.

Neck and Head: Base with B. Highlight where shown with W.

Chin strap: Base / W. Shade / VDB.

Eye: Base / B. Highlight / W as shown on Placement 2. Touch a tiny outline of W partially around eye. If it becomes too visible, blend edges into dark basecoat.

Bill: Base / B. Highlight / W.

Leg: Base / B. Highlight / W. Detail lines shown on design with B.

GRASSES:

Base / CYL + B, mixed to make a medium green. Shade with a little of that mixture + B where shown on Placement 2. HL / CYL + W.

SEEDS:

Apply thinned BS with point of round brush for grass seeds. Do not apply all the way to center stem and make seeds on stem ends smaller.

The Canada Goose

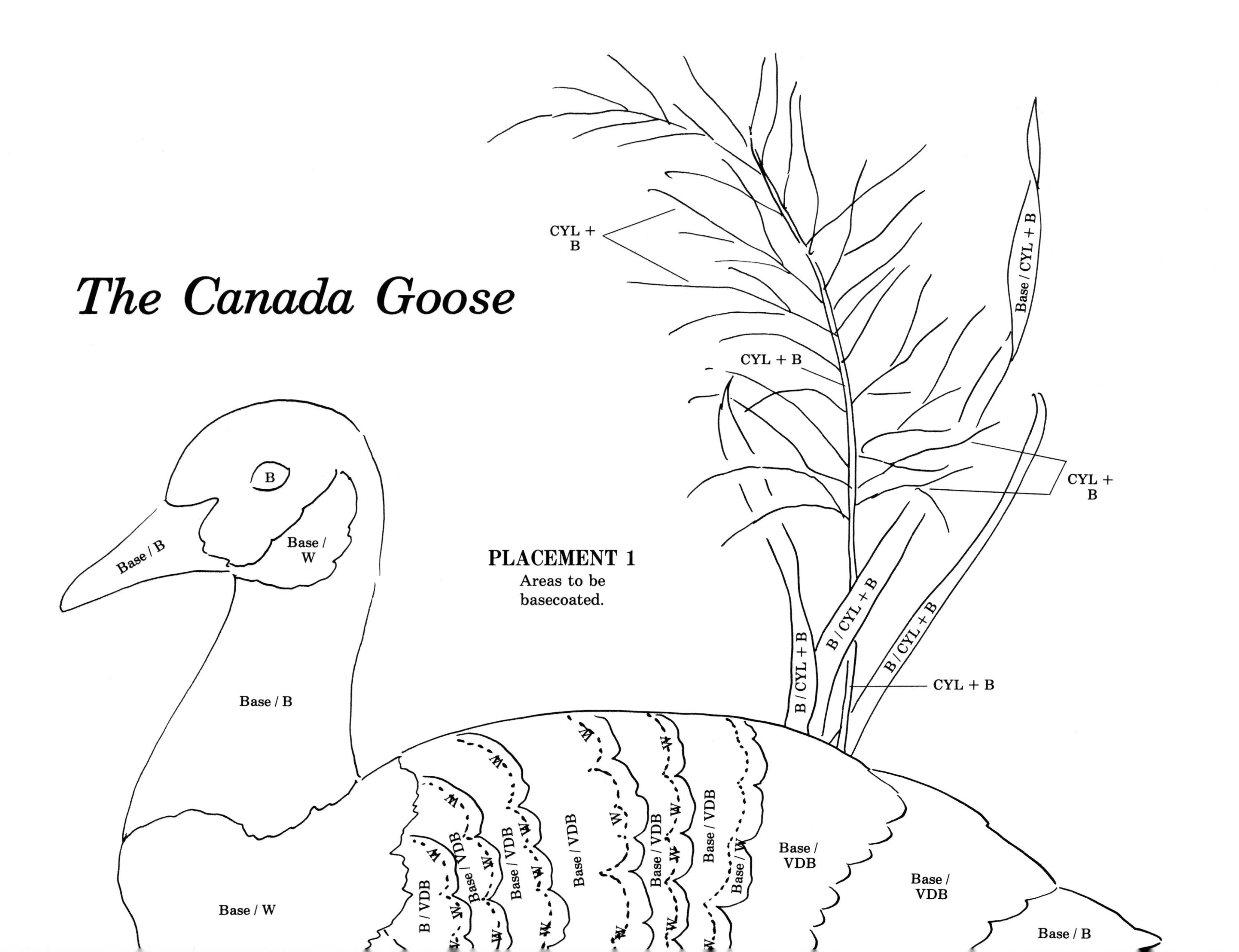

PLACEMENT 1
Areas to be basecoated.

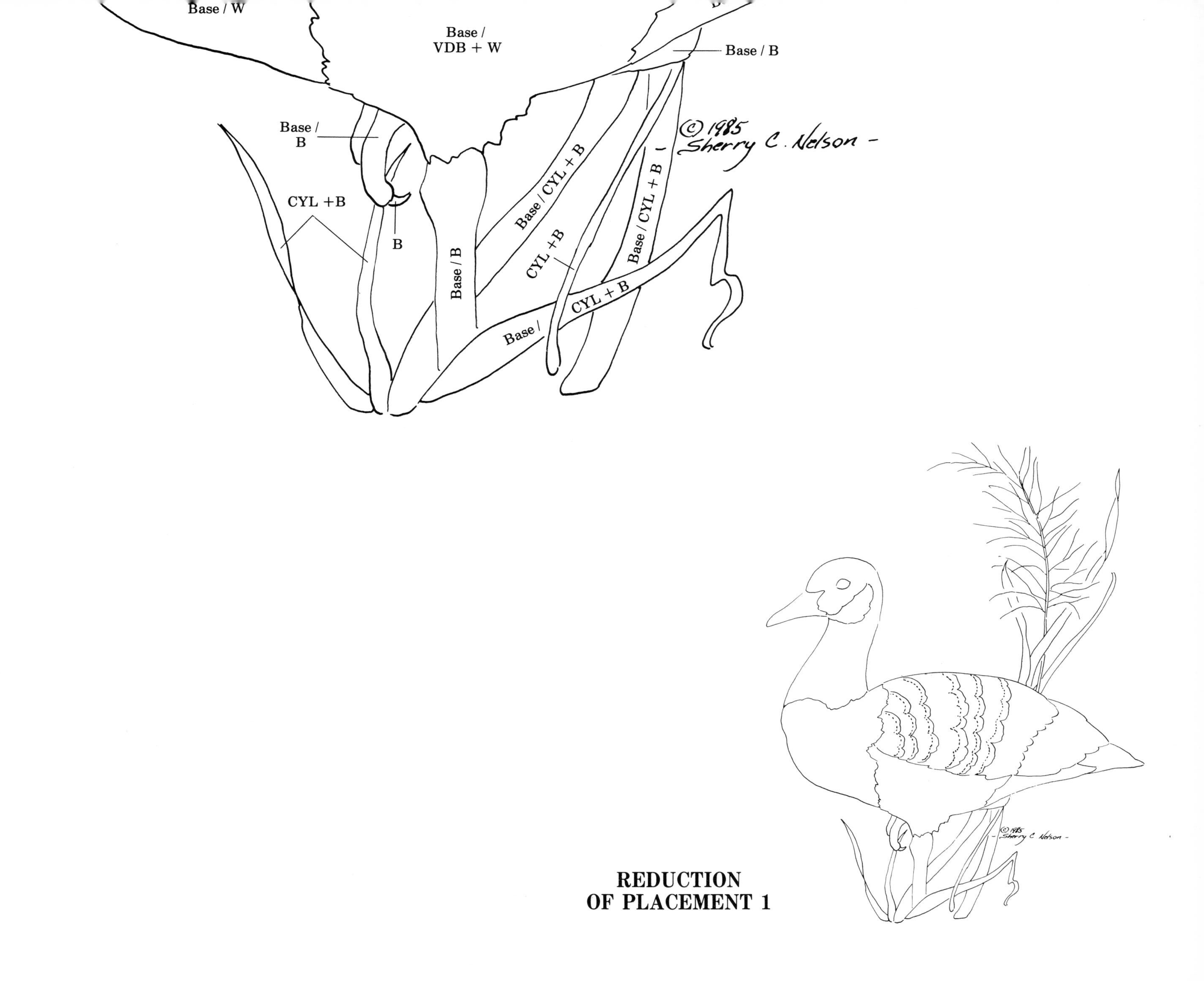

REDUCTION
OF PLACEMENT 1

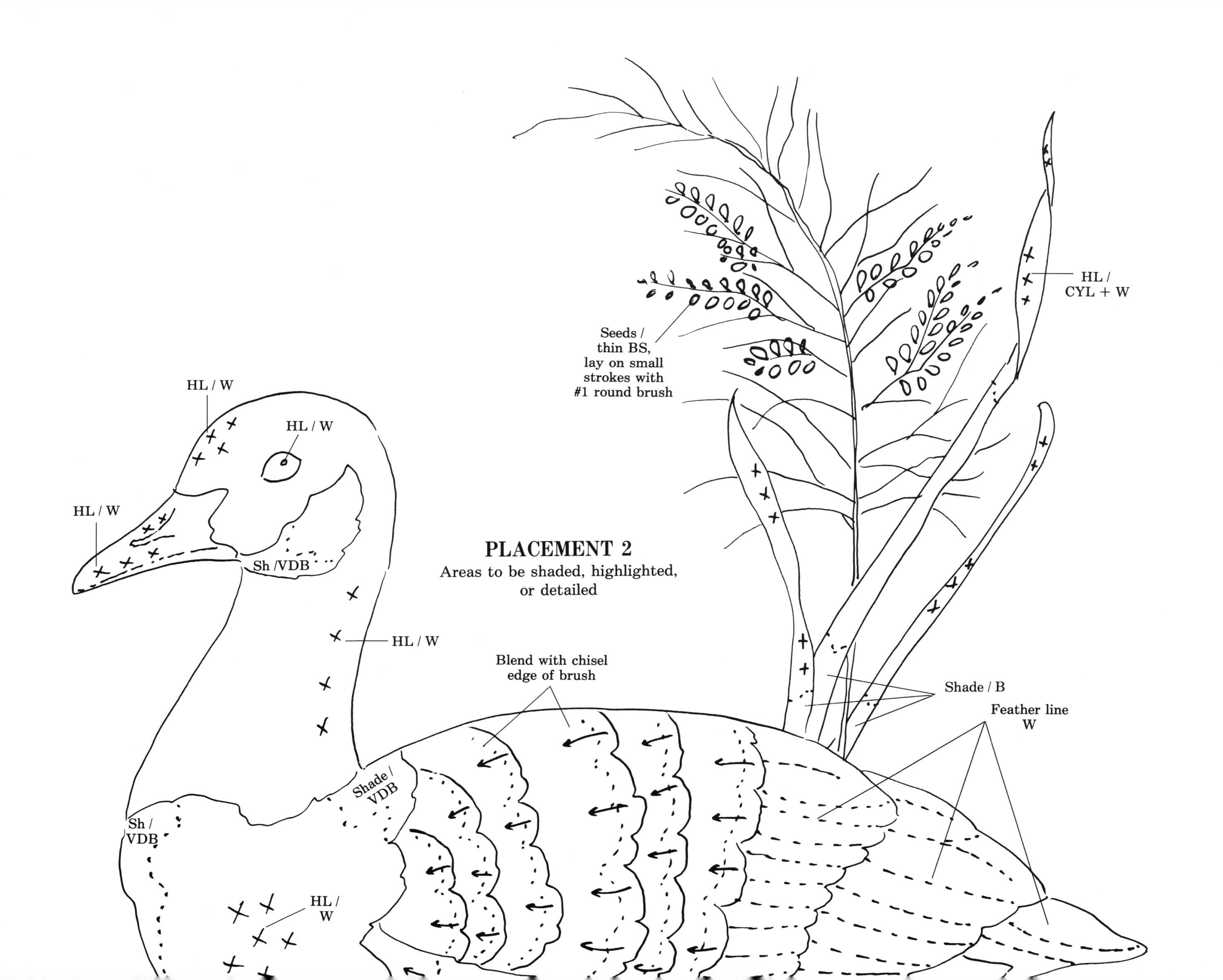

PLACEMENT 2
Areas to be shaded, highlighted, or detailed
Seeds / thin BS, lay on small strokes with #1 round brush
HL / CYL + W
HL / W
HL / W
HL / W
Sh /VDB
HL / W
Blend with chisel edge of brush
Shade / B
Feather line W
Shade / VDB
Sh / VDB
HL / W

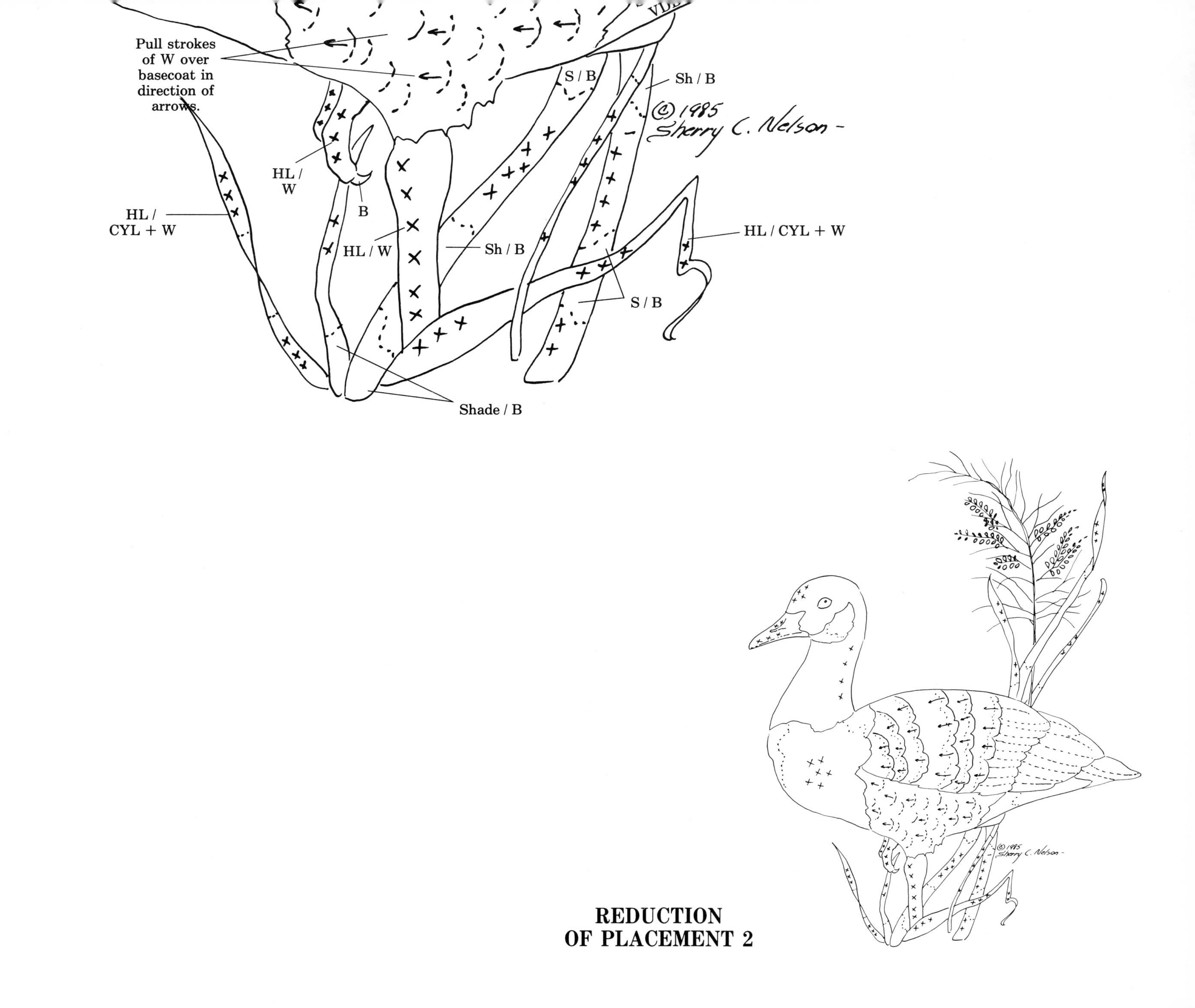

REDUCTION
OF PLACEMENT 2

Ring-billed Gull

Seagulls are one of the most difficult identification problems in the world of birds and this Ring-billed Gull is no exception. It is called a "three year gull" which means that it molts through a new and different plumage in each of its first three winters, with summer plumage varying slightly even from the winter. The ring on the bill is acquired when the bird is an adult and the Ring-billed Gull of our design is an adult bird. Next time you are at the beach, take a look at the tremendous variation between gulls—and you will understand why its difficult to know exactly which of the several common species you might be seeing. Regardless, they are graceful flyers and a delight to watch—the day at the shore would not be the same without them.

The background panel, size 11″×14″, is painted with sky blue acrylic paint. Brush on—or use a stencil roller for a slight texture and when dry spray with matte acrylic. The only color used to add background interest is W, applied with flat brush and rubbed out softly with cheesecloth to simulate high, light clouds. When dry, respray. Apply design with Artist's graphite.

Pictured in color on page 30.

Transfer this design to painting surface.

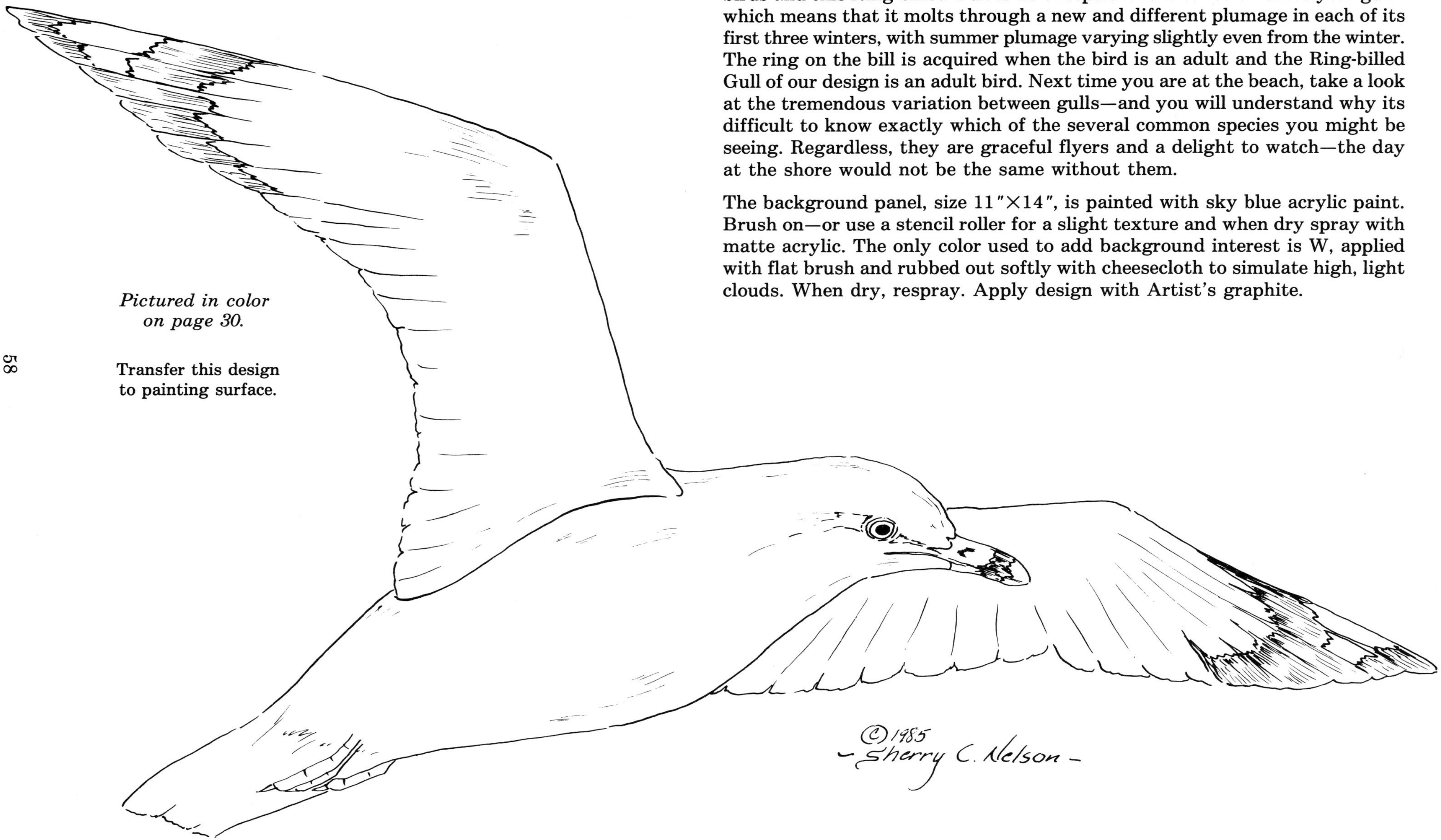

The colors used for this design are the following: Cadmium Yellow Medium, Raw Umber, Ivory Black, Titanium White, Ultramarine Blue and Raw Sienna.

Brushes: #8 bright and #1 round.

RING-BILLED GULL

Tail, body and head: Base / W + CYM, a pale mix with just a hint of warmth from the yellow. Shade where indicated on Placement 2 with RU + W or RU + UB + W. The shading color should be a medium value and the blue mix should not have too much blue in it. Blend in shading colors gently. Highlight with W in areas of xx's, and on tail pull some strokes with W on #8 brush to indicate feathers.

Eye: Pupil is based with B. Outline pupil with CYM for iris and add just a narrow outline around that with B. Highlight with W. Using a pointed brush will make this step a bit easier. Take your time!

PLACEMENT 1

Areas to be basecoated.

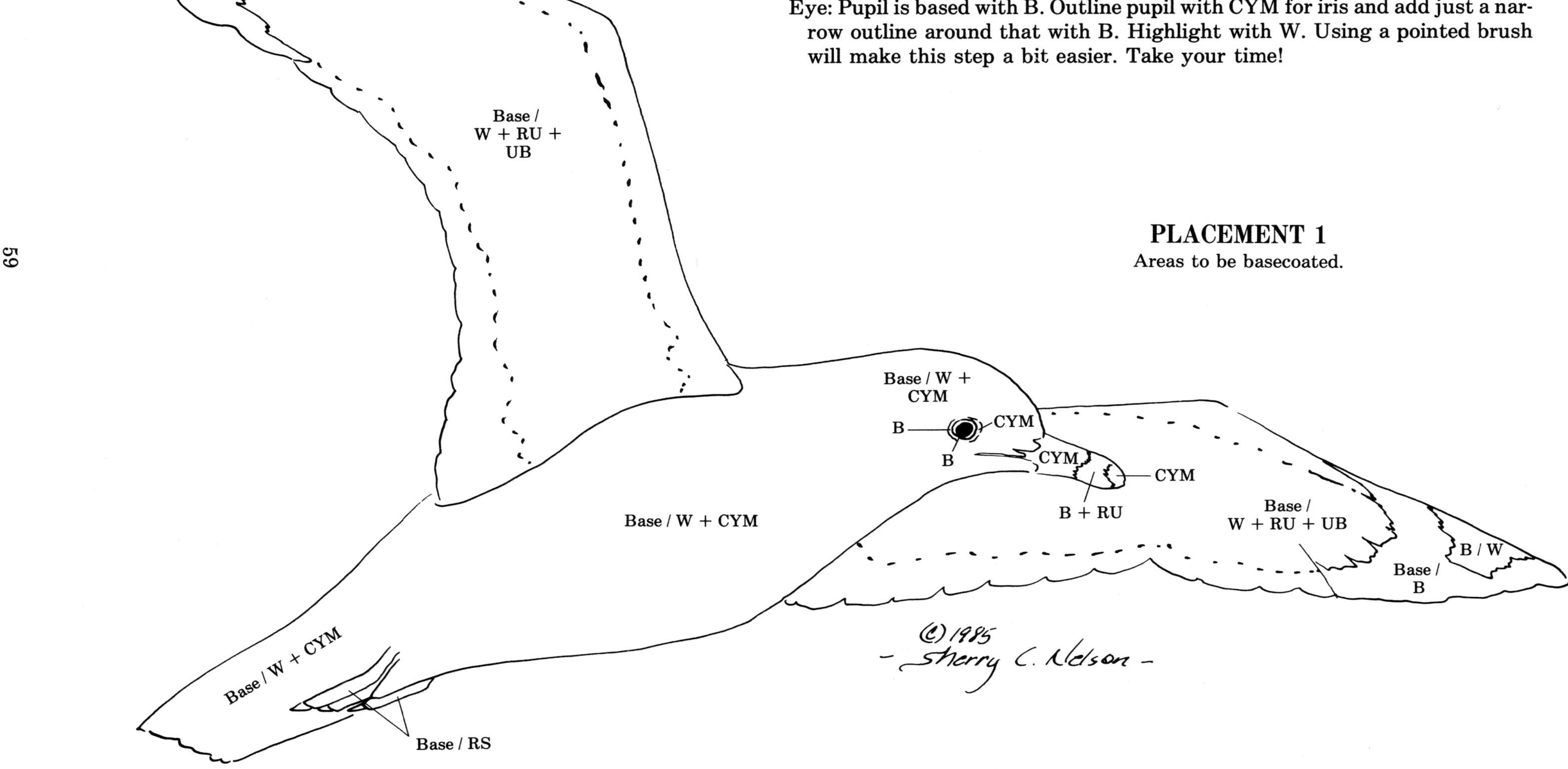

Ring-billed Gull

Beak: Base / CYM except in area of ring. Shade lower third of beak with RS, deepen in nostril area with RS and extend streak behind beak into cheek line with RS. Add "ring" with B + RU, blending just a little with chisel edge of bright into CYM areas.

Wingtips: Base wing tips with B, W according to placement sheet, Pull feather lines into each area with color shown on placement 2.

Wing: Base central area as shown with W + RU + UB. Color of mix should be a mid-value gray. Use chisel edge of brush to blend this area into wingtip color. Then pull feather strokes from both sides of wing in direction of arrows with W. If it becomes too textured, blend some of the W into the central wing area before proceding. W on brush should be dry; if brush is too heavy with paint, strokes will be too obvious on wing.

Legs: Base / RS. Highlight / CYM + W. Then add detail lines with RS on round brush and toenails with RU.

PLACEMENT 2

Areas to be shaded & highlighted.

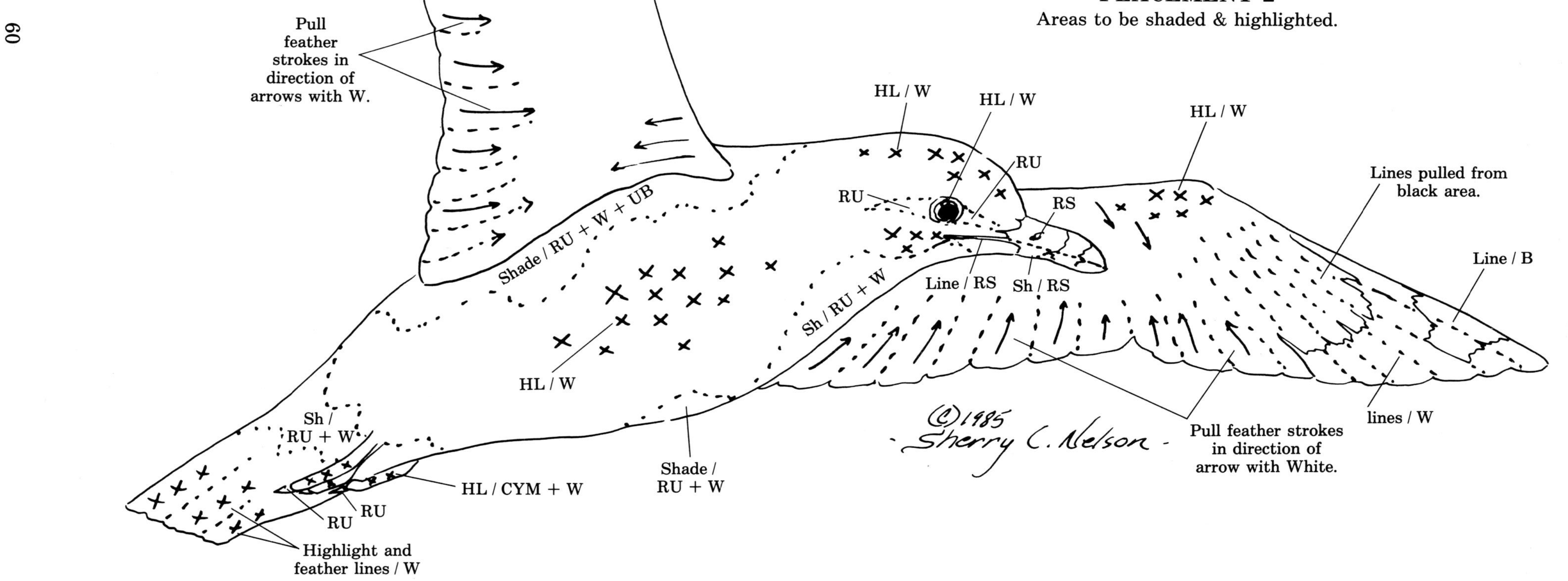

Transfer this
design to painting surface.

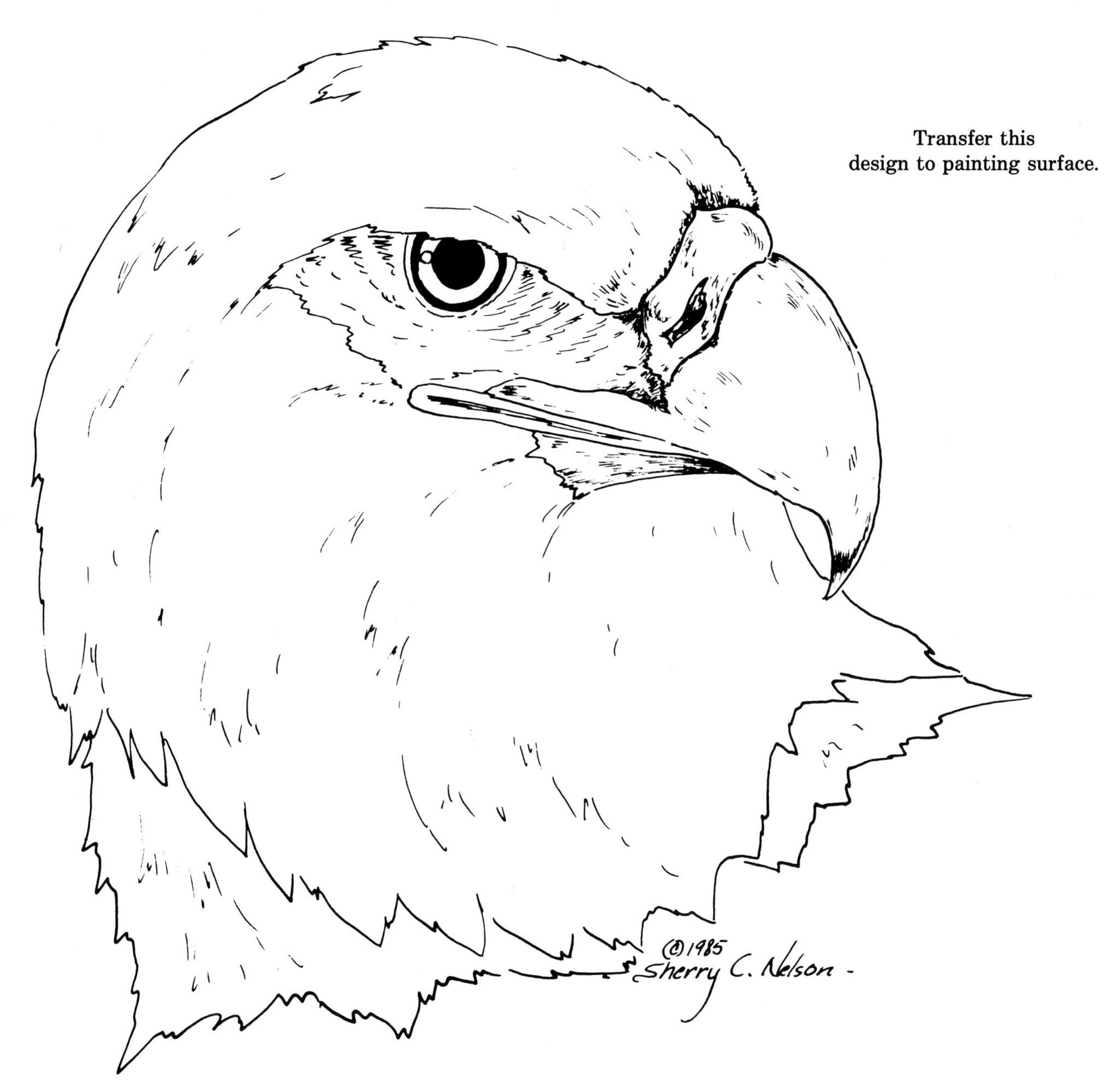

Pictured in color on page 31.

The Bald Eagle

Our National bird—and symbol of the grandeur and majesty that is America . . . there is hardly a person that does not recognize the American Eagle. This dramatic portrait shows the fully adult eagle with the snowy white feathers of crown and head as well as the massive golden bill. It takes the Bald Eagle 5 full years to reach adult plumage; for the first four years of its life it is a rich brown bird with white underwing patterning. The Bald Eagle is predominantly a fish eater and usually found on seacoasts, rivers and lakes. The birds have been seriously diminished in numbers due to illegal shooting, pesticides and loss of habitat, but recovery programs have helped to stabilize the population in the Eastern United States.

The background is an 8″×10″ piece of masonite, painted with soft gray acrylic paint and sprayed with matte finish acrylic spray. The out-of-focus background colors, added according to instructions given in the foreword, are RU, WG and W. Rub the oils into the background with a soft cloth, let dry and respray. Then apply design with Artist's graphite.

The following colors are needed: Raw Sienna, Raw Umber, Ivory Black, Titanium White, Chrome Yellow Deep, and Cadmium Yellow Light.

You will need a #8 bright and a #1 round brush for this design.

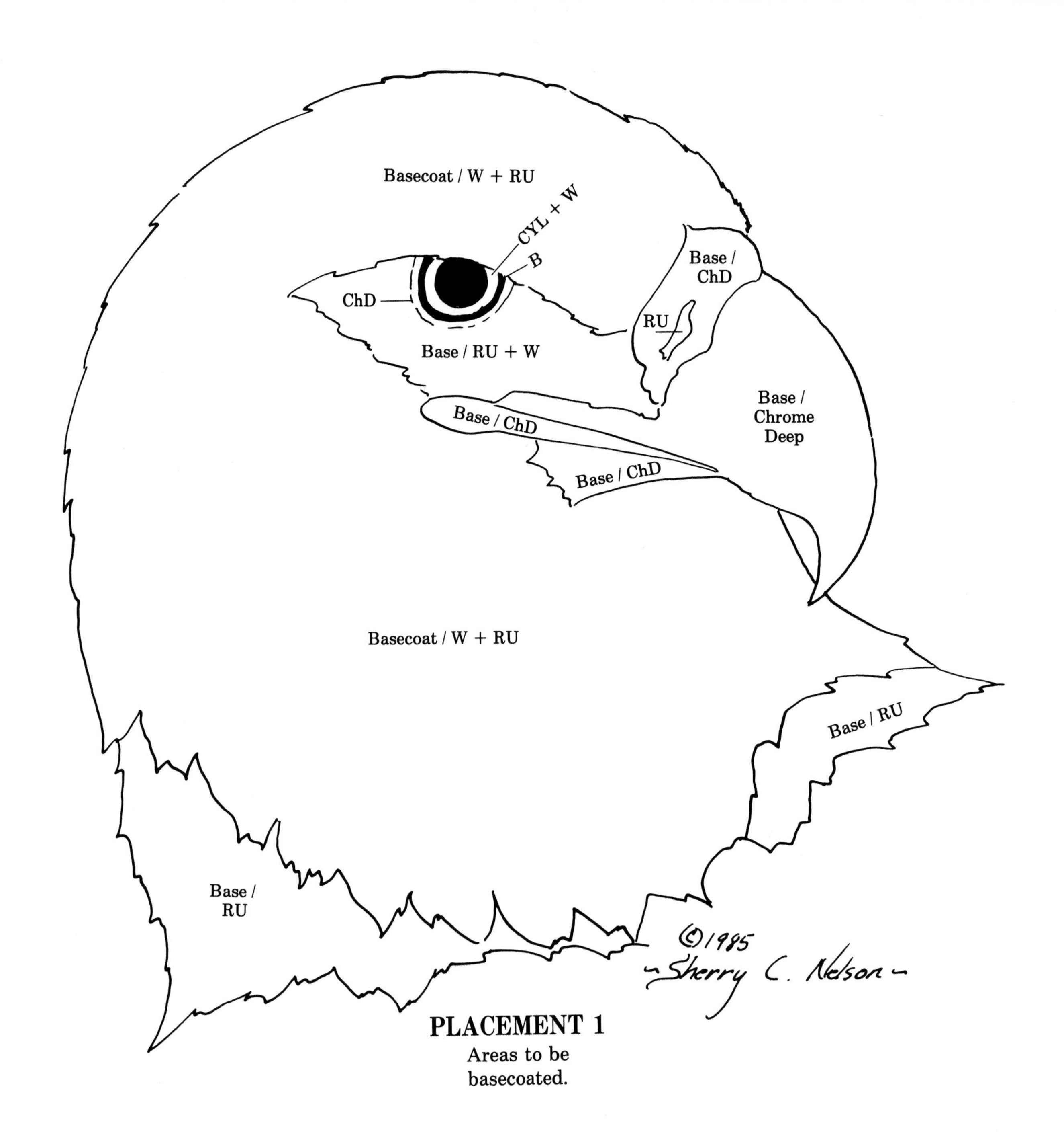

PLACEMENT 1
Areas to be basecoated.

The Bald Eagle

THE EAGLE
Neck feathers: Base / RU.
Head: Base / W + RU. Use very little RU in the mixture, so that the basecolor is an off-white with just a gray cast to it. Base sparsely, even though it will take some time. If you apply the white paint too heavily, you will have difficulty with shading and highlight areas.

Around eye, base with a slightly darker mixture of W + RU, as shown on placement 1. Blend this area just slightly into the lighter basecoat to the left of it. Do not blend where it meets the lighter color along brow line.

Shade where indicated on Placement 2 with RU. Blend carefully into basecoat. Highlight / W in areas of xx's. Add W detailing with W on round brush to obtain texture.

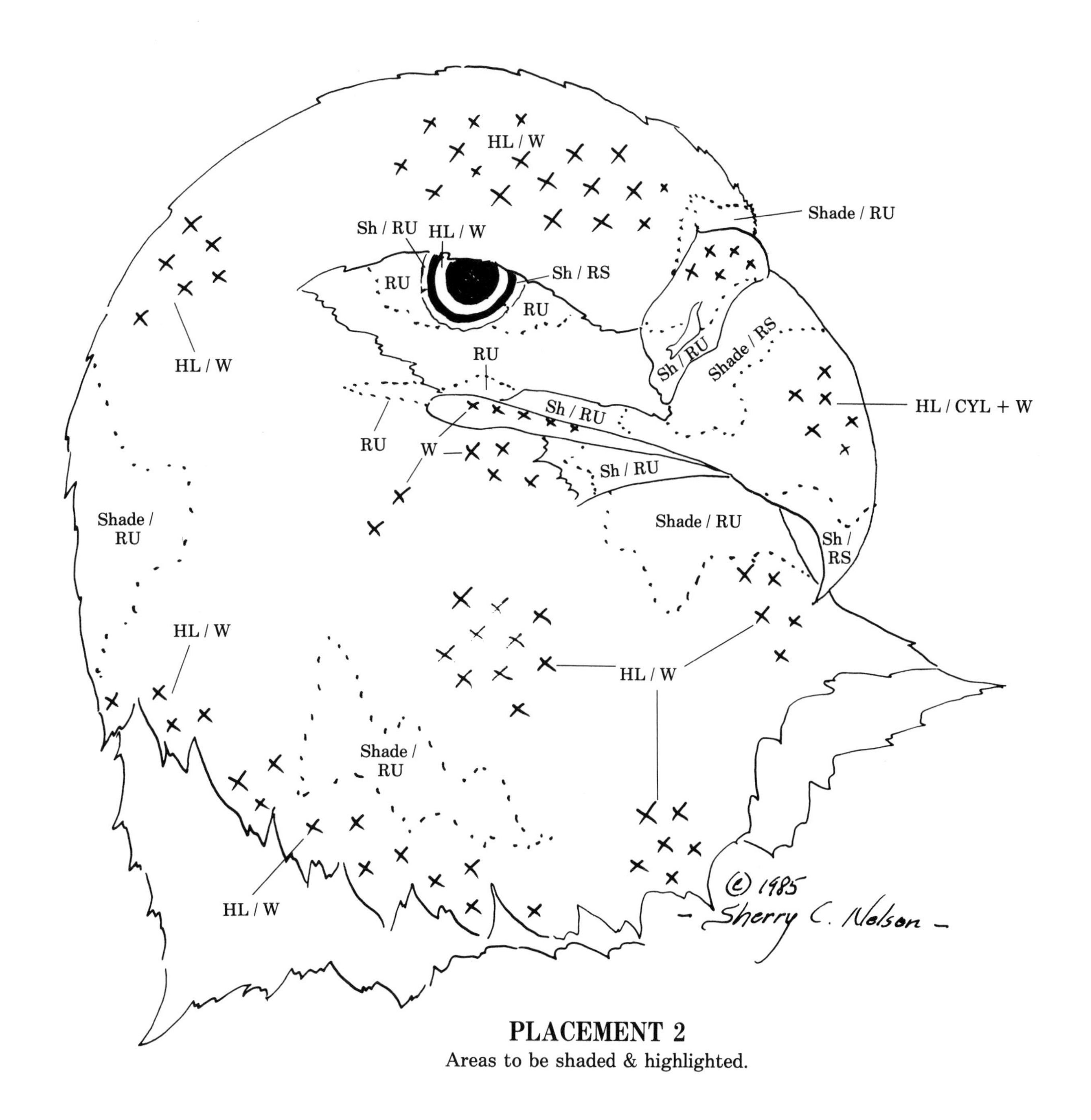

PLACEMENT 2
Areas to be shaded & highlighted.

Shade with RU at corners of eye where indicated. Add RU detailing around eye as shown on design with round brush.

Bill: Base / ChD. Shade with either RS or RU as indicated. Highlight with first CYL and then CYL + W where shown with xx's. Add nostril depression with RU.

Eye: First fill in pupil with B. Then carefully, with pointed brush, fill in iris with CYL + W. Shade just a tiny bit at upper corners of iris with RU. Add highlight dot with W.

Outline iris with fine line of B, using round brush. Outline around black line with ChD, using round brush.

Take your time when doing the eye. Remember, with B and CYL combining to make green, the eye could very quickly turn into a problem. If color smudges occur, remove with brush dampened in turp.

A Last Word . . .

It has been my pleasure sharing with you what I love best—birds and bird painting. I hope you have enjoyed every single bird—on every single page.

I have tried to make this book truly basic and to help the entry-level painter develop skill and confidence. I truly hope that YOU have found it helpful and enjoyable.

Questions? Comments? Successes to share? Let me hear from you!

Sherry C. Nelson
The MAGIC BRUSH, INC.
P.O. Box 868
Anthony, TX/NM 88021